For Winners/For Losers is trademark pending with the United States Patent and Trademark office.

First printing June 2023

Library of Congress Cataloging-in-Publication Data

Scott, Eli

ten wealth principles for losers / by eli scott

Paperback ISBN: 979-8-9872758-3-2

Squishy Publishing

Interior Design by Eva Myrick, MSCP

Ten Wealth Principles For Losers™

by Eli Scott

**Squishy
Publishing**

DISCLAIMER

This book does not provide or guarantee employment, success, or results in any business, career, or investment. Individual results vary. In addition, caution should be taken against risks involved in any business or investment opportunity and we suggest seeking legal, financial, and business consult with any pursuit.

This book is intended for educational and informational purposes only in career and financial wellbeing. You nevertheless need to know that your ultimate success or failure will be the result of your own efforts, your particular situation, and innumerable other circumstances that extend beyond the scope of this book.

The information and/or documents contained in this book do not constitute legal, financial, or investment advice including that of credit analysis and should never be used without first consulting with a financial professional to determine what may be best for your individual needs.

The publisher and the author do not make any guarantee or other promise as to any results that may be obtained from using the content of this book. You should never make any investment decision without first consulting with your own financial advisor and conducting your own research and due diligence. To the maximum extent permitted by law, the publisher and the author disclaim any and all liability in the event that any information, commentary, analysis, opinions, advice and/or recommendations contained in this book prove to be inaccurate, incomplete or unreliable, or result in any investment loss or other losses.

The publisher and the author are providing this book and its contents on an "as is" basis. Your use of the information in this book is at your own risk.

Past performance of investments are not a guarantee of future results. Each investment decision you make should be made in reference to the specific information available for that investment at the time of so choosing as well as under legal guidance and not based on past recommendations.

Making adjustments to a financial strategy or plan should only be undertaken after consulting with a professional. The publisher and the author make no guarantee of financial results obtained by using this book.

Eli Scott |

Acknowledgements

I know most people aren't going to read this section anyways and so I'm going to keep this short. Overall, I would like to thank my dad for everything he did for me to make my writing ventures possible in every way. I would like to thank all of my friends who have been so supportive of me in every way. You all know who you are. Finally, I would like thank my loving fiancé, MC. Thank you for all of your enthusiasm in my books and being my number one fan. You are everything to me and may nothing ever pull us apart.

Eli Scott |

Eli Scott |

Introduction

The only person you are destined to become is the person you decide to be. -Ralph Waldo Emerson

I first gained the burning passion many years ago at the age of twenty seven to write a series of books on money and wealth when I stumbled across a series of other get rich books from the likes of Robert Kiyosaki, Toni Robbins, and T. Harv Eker who wrote Secrets of a Millionaire Mind, which I must have read over one hundred times. It was mostly through this last book that influenced me to start my career in personal wealth book writing and more importantly the no non-sense attitude that I needed to become wealthy. And that is exactly what this particular book is about, is the no non-sense attitude that you must have, and the things you must do and practice daily if you want to become wealthy someday.

Now wait a second? Isn't this book titled Ten Wealth Principles... *For Losers?* Yes, this is a book for the losers, not as in people who are losers, but the ones who were not born into money. We are the ones who don't have the means to become wealthy, but seek the ways that we too can become wealthy. But, and this is a BIG but... this book is not for just anyone. This book is not for those who are not willing to do what it takes to become wealthy because you can't get rich by simply wishing for and sitting on it. One can have a dream and a goal, as well as a wealth avenue, but you also must have this other half of the formula in the behaviors, habits, attitudes, lifestyle, and discipline you must have to manifest your dreams for you.

This book also does not contain the means to become wealthy. If that is what you are looking for, then you can resort to my other book series Think and Be Rich and The Portal to Financial Gold and Think and Be Rich and the Portal to Online Gold which provide personal wealth and money-making systems for you.

A few other things I want to mention are that there are many places in this book where I reference my other books. This is not intended to promote those books but to cite them so as not to commit self-plagiarism. I also want to define entrepreneurship here. These days, it seems like there are many definitions for what an entrepreneur is. When I'm using the term entrepreneur in this book, I am referring to anyone who hustles to build their own personal wealth system in any number of income streams to include side hustles, real estate, inventing a new or improved product, founding a company, becoming a business partner, being self-employed, starting a small business, owning a franchise, to being a best-selling author, big investor, being employed in a career that pays high wages or any other type of money making systems. Also, anytime I refer to "rich people" in this book, I am referring to those who get rich from the bottom and not those who were born into money or inherited money. Anytime I use the term chapters, I am referring to wealth principles as this book doesn't have chapters, and so the terms are interchangeable with one another. Finally, this book is not written perfectly, and it's not meant to be. It's simply meant to get the concepts across in helping you to become rich and wealthy.

I would also like to mention that I didn't have to write this book in order to make money. I am not desperate in becoming rich through any book sales as I have already found my way to become well off which I will go over with you. So then why did I choose to publish my books? The honest answer to this is that yes, I did at one point use my book writing as a potential money-making avenue until I was able to find other ways to leverage my money. By the time I had found success through these other avenues, all of my books were already mostly written. With all of the hard work that I put into them, it would have been a waste to not publish them. However, I also love educating and I want to help people. Why? Because I know what it's like to be born into poverty and to struggle. More importantly, I want to help fight these giant financial predators who are preying on poor and desperate people in this world with their predatory financial policies and investment opportunities and if there is one thing that people can get out of my books that will help them then I did something good in this world.

Although this is called Ten Wealth Principles For Losers, you will find that this book has more than twenty* as well as bonus material that can turn whoever is willing to follow them from average losers into mega winning "lottery" winners ahead. Along with that, you will need to make the decision right now to change your life forever. To make the decision now means to not sit on it and to follow the steps that I will provide to you for as long as it takes to build your wealthy empire. It doesn't have to take forever to become wealthy. You can achieve your wealthy success within the next two to five years if you follow through every single day on what it takes to get there. If you are, however, one of the few people who is willing to do what no one else will to become wealthy, then I now invite you to the Ten Wealth Principles For Losers ahead.

To your happiness, prosperity, and success.

Eli Scott

* Why did I title this the way that I did? From a marketing standpoint it just sounds more appealing to call this ten wealth principles instead of twenty which would not be as sellable to people. We will go over a few simple but powerful marketing techniques that can help you with you to build wealth in your money making systems in one of the chapters.

Eli Scott |

Wealth Principle 1

You must think rich to be rich

He is able who thinks he is able. - Siddhartha Gautama, the Buddha

While this is one of the shortest wealth principles in this book, it will also be the most powerful in becoming rich or amassing millions of dollars to you in which it cannot be underestimated and that is: you must think rich to be rich. What do I mean by that? What I mean is that you must not stop thinking about or in some cases, even obsessing about becoming rich. Now I know some of you might say that's not normal or healthy to obsess over anything in which I say rich people do not live normal lives and only focus on becoming wealthy as I will go over more in another wealth principle ahead.

You must make becoming rich your life focus and your number one goal and priority. You must be stubborn and persistent in your unending thoughts and actions to do what it takes every single second of every single day from sun up to sun down for the next ten to twenty years or however long it takes that you are going to be rich someday even if you don't know how. You don't have to worry about how it's going to happen, but it is this persisting belief and attitude that will carry you through as you work your butt off figuring out how you are going to make that happen and doing whatever it is you do that will make you that rich millionaire someday.

So what does this stubborn mindset look like? This looks like the words "I will be rich" plastered onto your forehead with the unlimiting beliefs that will drive you every day towards your goal to become rich. And more importantly, you must have this stubborn goal and belief that you will become filthy rich no matter how long it takes, no matter how many times you fail, and no matter your age in the process of doing so. It has been said many times over that most millionaires don't become millionaires until after the age of forty or fifty. I am not saying that you shouldn't become a millionaire at the age of twenty if you have the means to do so, but what I am saying is that you need to start with this goal and work towards it as early in life as possible and not stop working at it until you see your millionaire success come to you. Hopefully it won't take you that long to become a millionaire in which my Think and Be Rich book series can help you to achieve faster, but those who are dead serious on becoming wealthy will not let anything stop them.

Throughout my many years of attempting to become rich, I found myself coming home many nights on end year after year over a twenty year period in my attempts to become rich and yet I didn't let any failure stop me from pursuing further. Furthermore, I woke up every morning and went to bed every night with the persisting forethought that I was going to without a doubt be a rich millionaire someday. And it was that forethought that drove me to keep working at it every day of my life to persist in my path to become a mega millionaire. Furthermore, I did anything and everything I needed to in order to figure out how I was going to get there from reading books on how to get rich to studying different get rich endeavors that would someday shower me with millions of dollars. But I couldn't have done it without the persisting attitude and thought every single second of every single day that I was going to be mega rich someday and that I was going to put in all of the hard work and do whatever it took to get there. It was with my continued efforts day after day for twenty years that I suddenly was able to put everything I had attempted and learned together that it was like a magical fire exploded one day that would eventually be the ONE thing that would build my wealth empire.

So why is this stubborn and persistent forethought so important in your path to becoming wealthy? There are two reasons why this is the most important step in your wealth path and that is you are what you eat and believing in yourself or not listening to others. While I will go over not listening to others in wealth principle number three, I want to focus on you are what you eat in this chapter. Although I do think that your health and nutrition is important to giving you energy and a clear and positive mind to amassing your millions of dollars, I am not talking about the food you eat in this wealth principle here. So now, what do I mean by you are what you eat? The difference between staying poor or becoming rich drills down to what you think and focus on as well as what you believe you are capable of doing.

When you look at everyone around you in your life from your parents to your neighbors, your teachers, friends, family, and acquaintances, ask yourself what it is about them that they are not rich? If anyone can become rich, why aren't they? The answer to this question is that not just *anyone* can become rich and wealthy, and that is because getting rich and wealthy is not what they ever think about. Becoming rich is not their life goal, is not something that they strive for, and is not something that they believe can be real for them or that they are ever capable of achieving, which is one of the biggest things that stops people from moving further.

You have to make getting rich your number one goal every single second of every single day for the rest of your life first and second, you need to have the mindset that getting rich is as real as the sun rising and falling everyday and that it can happen for you, that you are *capable* of becoming rich like any other rich person. By doing these two things, you will then strive for the careers, business enterprises, investments and other endeavors that will make you rich. See the difference between that and smart people around you? I am not saying that smart people can't become rich because they can and many of them do if they find ways to leverage or multiply their money. I am also not meaning to degrade or insult smart people who I highly admire and respect. The point of this is to compare those who focus on their wealth versus those who don't. Those who are not rich and never will be are the ones who focus on going to a job everyday and serving a mission to their communities, collecting a paycheck, and then going home to their children. Now there's nothing wrong with that either but again they don't focus on the things and endeavors that will make them rich and that is what you will have to do in order to become rich, to never stop thinking it in which you will then be steered on the paths that will. In other words, you have to make becoming rich your essence of being and a way of life for you.

Now don't worry yet as to how you are going to do this or how you are going to adopt this new lifestyle as the rest of the principles in this book will help you to do what you need to in order to become wealthy. But before we get to those things, we must first discuss gaining the right get rich mentality that you too can become wealthy ahead.

Eli Scott |

Wealth Principle 2

You too can become wealthy

The greatest pleasure in life is doing what people say you cannot do.
- Walter Bagehot

If there is any one thing that stops most people from becoming wealthy, it is in that of people who don't set their mind to it and furthermore, separate themselves from rich and wealthy people in which they don't think of it as something that is real or possible for them as we discussed in the first wealth principle. To really get my point across with this one, the general public is taught and engrained with the mindset set forth by their parents, teachers, neighbors, employers, co-workers, and friends as to what is real and what is "normal" in our day to day lives that stop us from doing whatever we set out to do in our get rich dreams and desires.

We are instead taught to do what *is* defined as normal and real by our society and that is we go to school to become nurses or teachers or to go get a normal job somewhere but we aren't taught to think outside of that to form into people who are capable of becoming millionaires because that's not normal and furthermore, we are shamed for even trying to aspire at any of these things and told that we will fail and to go do something *real* in our jobs, careers, and endeavors. Furthermore, all of these same people want to define us and tell us who we can and can't be or what we can or can't do.

I'm here to tell you that it is you and only you who can determine who you are and what is possible within you and it is up to you to do unto you. In other words, you are the one who has to break past all of these people who tell you that getting rich isn't real and to form the mindset that getting rich is in fact real and that it's possible for you if you are willing to do that it takes to get there. You need to pursue your wealth path on your own without any of those people and regardless of what they are doing or what they think about you in the process and live by the same motto as I do which I was so proud to put on my social media accounts one day after all of my hard work which says:

"I am so happy that I never let anyone tell me who to be, what to do, or how to live, because now I get to live the life that no one else does!"

Now of course you might think you know what it means to not let others define you or tell you what to do, but I had to take this motto to the extreme and so here is what it meant for me. For me, not letting others define me or tell me who to be, what to do, or how to live meant not getting married or having children until after I was way older, quitting my job and selling my house for a profit, renting out a bedroom in my parent's house while I slept on an air mattress, and working as a pizza delivery driver for four years while I worked through my endeavors. I'm not telling you to do any of these things as everyone has different journeys in their lives, but what I am saying is that these were the things I felt like I needed to do to achieve my wealthy desires. The point is, you too may find yourself going through extremes in what it takes to become wealthy and you don't let people tell you who to be, how to live, and what to do if you want to bring fortune to you. No one defines you or determines the path that you will take in life but you. When other people want to tear you down as to what is not real, that is what is not real for them and what will never be real for them but they are not you and they don't trek the same path that you do in your millionaire enterprises. Furthermore, those people hold the mindset that they are obligated to their ball and chain nine to five job everyday and then have their other life obligations to distract them.

In addition to breaking past all of these people, you also need to break past all of your doubts and obstacles in becoming rich a reality for you. So now what doubts and obstacles do I speak of? In my book Think and Be Rich and the Portal to Financial Gold, I have a chapter titled the road to wealthy success which explains how we are engrained with the beliefs that we are pre-determined by what we are supposed to do. We are rooted with the mindset that we must wake up to the same alarm clock to go to the same job that we are obligated to everyday. We furthermore get distracted by the highs and lows of the beauties and pleasures in life that can numb us everyday and keep us from focusing on our dreams and desires. Finally, we don't think that becoming rich is real because we don't see anyone else doing the same things as us in achieving our wealth to us. If you want to become rich however, you cannot let the comforts of life blind or stop you from pursuing your wealth for you. You have to maintain the stubborn mindset that you too can have it someday and that you will move past all of these obstacles to achieve greatness for you. We will also discuss breaking past your limited beliefs to not be defined by a nine to five job to pursue your wealth in another chapter.

Now just as important as seeing that wealth can be real for you, you also need to realize that you are just as deserving and worthy of becoming rich as any other rich person. If you don't feel deserving or worthy of it then let me ask you this: Do you feel bad when your employer wants to pay you only thirty thousand dollars a year with a one thousand dollar bonus every two years at a job that requires a difficult college degree or licenses as well as ten years of experience? Do you feel bad when your boss comes up with lies as to how you didn't perform your job right so that he can steal your bonus from you every year to put into his own bank account? And do you feel bad when your employer lays you off first as a top performing employee after being loyal to your job for ten to fifteen years so that he doesn't have to give you your deserved raises? While there are many younger readers here who don't believe me on these astonishing things, us older people know the reality of these awful ways that employers treat us.

There are even companies who hire consultants to form creative ways to trick employees out of their yearly bonuses and raises, and they will back up their claims to your poor performance with the "hundreds" of complaints against you that don't even exist. Additionally, it has been said that wage theft by employers to include bonuses and raises is one of the most committed crimes in America reportedly in the range of fifty billion dollars. Let me say that again. Employers are reportedly stealing fifty billion dollars from their employees across America! There are also many agencies who blame stagnant wages as one of the leading causes of homelessness in America. Additionally, there is about ninety-five billion US dollars in retail theft in America every year resulting in again decreased wages and inflated prices. So, if you want to accept your stagnant wages at your job every year that you can't make ends meet with then you can have it. For the rest of us, making a lot of money is nothing more than just being able to pay our bills and figuring out how to keep our earned profits that no one can steal from us!

Additionally, when you think about it, your money does not belong to you. Your money belongs to your spouse or ex-spouse, your money belongs to your kids, your money belongs to your mortgage and debt, your money belongs to the IRS, your money belongs to money grubbing capitalists, your money belongs to the oil industry, your money belongs to all of your bills, credit cards, loans and debt, your money belongs to finance companies, and your money belongs to your employer. Your money belongs to everyone else but you and to the rich. How do you think rich people get and stay rich? From everyone else's money! So when you really think about it, you don't even own your own working hours. Society owns you and your hours and if you don't learn how to leverage or multiply your money, then you are nothing more than glorified slave trade where everyone else owns you. How do I know? Calculate how much money you have made over the last twenty years and how much you have in your bank account now in which the difference will be astonishing. It is known that the majority of people don't even have ten thousand dollars in savings after having worked for the past twenty years and most people also lose money on their investments. This is not about any conspiracy theories. I don't believe in conspiracy theories and anytime people around me bring them up, I just roll my eyes at them. I'm simply pointing out real facts to help you not feel guilty about wanting to make a lot of money.

You also need to not let guilt from other people's struggles stop you in becoming wealthy. You need not be concerned with other people's financial problems and focus on your deservingness in becoming rich. To relieve your guilt, ask yourself, what it is that you do to help people? I help people by writing books on personal wealth in which I receive royalties back for the hundreds of thousands of hours I put into this over a twenty year period. Do I feel bad about the money I receive back for it? Heck no, because I slaved away for it and this is what I do to make a decent living in this world where we need a healthy paycheck to survive. Additionally, the steep sacrifices that I made to find wealth were so severe that I would not in the least feel guilted into giving my money away to those who didn't go through the pain that I did to earn it. I'm not saying I don't donate to good causes. I do donate a lot of time to volunteer work and money to good causes. What I'm saying is I don't feel guilted into simply giving handouts to people who did nothing for the money that I rightfully earned and that I know my deservingness in earning a lot of money. It's up to you to know what your deservingness is of receiving your well earned money especially if you work hard for your money!

Now that we have gone over your deservingness in becoming rich and that it can be real for you, we now move onto the next wealth principle in not listening to others in telling you what you can or can't do ahead.

Eli Scott |

Wealth Principle 3

Don't listen to others

Keep away from people who try to belittle your ambitions. Small people always do that, but the really great make you feel that you, too, can become great. -Mark Twain

One of the most important things to do when it comes to chasing after money is not listening to others in what you can and cannot do. We all know that the people closest to us will be our biggest naysayers in which they all want to instill a lot of fear and doubt into you. And so you work hard to tear the brick walls down to make your dreams a reality for you and everyone around you quickly jumps their one hundred hands in to rebuild this brick wall that you just tore down. While poor people let others tell them what they can't do, rich people relentlessly ignore everyone around them and don't care what they think about them. We cannot determine or tell people what to do and it is not up to them to tell you what to do. You do you, and see yourself building your wealthfolio while ignoring everyone around you!

Follow the mantra that you are stronger, smarter, more stubborn, and that you will struggle to build your wealth so that you no longer have to struggle. Which brings me to another point that you need to be above any of these people who tear you down, to simply dodge and float above the negativity, and furthermore to be strong willed in your pursuit to become wealthy.

When your friends and family want to put that brick wall back up that you just tore down, you just simply jump over it or, better yet, run right through it!

You need to see that you are separate from all of these people and they will not build your wealth for you. So it is up to you to do what it takes to enterprise you regardless of anyone who wants to try to tear you down in the process. You need not care what people think and do even if you are the only one you know who is doing it and even if you don't know how you are going to become rich. You have to be ten percent smarter than all of your naysayers by knowing that you can and will make this happen with the stubborn will power that you are going to make it happen.

You need to hold the stubborn mindset against other people's negativity that you will become rich and that you will continue to do whatever it takes to get there. When you think about it, there is no one who is guaranteeing or protecting anyone's retirement plans, and no retirement plans of any sort have been known to stay in existence forever. It has also been said that most people will work until the day they die. Everyone no matter who they are will struggle in life to keep paying their bills and making a living and so you have to determine which struggle you want to take in life – that in which you are working for the rest of your life while losing all of the money you worked so hard for, or that in which you struggle ten times more in a shorter amount of time so that you no longer have to struggle? And finally, you have to be stronger than the negativity they throw at you to try to stop you from pursuing further and you pursue through it!

And so this is exactly the motto of the four S's that I had to follow with any of my doubters who told me what I could and couldn't do and to be above the negativity that your naysayers throw at you in which I said:

I am:

Stronger than you

Smarter than you, more

Stubborn than you and I will

Struggle so that I no longer have to struggle!

Of course you might be asking, why tell people at all about your goals and the things you are doing to become rich someday which is good advice - to just not tell people about it at all. However, some people are not able to hide their ambitions when people can see them actively working on them. Additionally, telling people about your ambitions can be beneficial as doing so sets your intentions of your goals. Those who either write or state their goals and intentions out loud significantly increase their chances of achieving them. Having accountability partners can also be powerful when they hold you to your word in doing what it is you said you would do. Telling people about your goals also has another gratifying benefit when you see the look on your naysayers faces someday as you say "I told you so", and, "don't ask me for help when all you wanted to do was try to tear me down by telling me what I couldn't do".

In addition to not listening to others, it is also important that we discuss other people's insulting and offensive criticism towards you. Of course I'm not talking about constructive criticism and positive feedback you will get from experts who you should certainly listen to. I am referring to those people who are only trying to stop you from doing anything at all and who are very unkind in demoralizing you in which you once again ignore them. You need to understand that most of the time you are receiving this criticism from people who don't know anything that they are talking about and are not someone worthy of listening to. A good way to think about this is to think of yourself as an employer who qualifies or disqualifies candidates by determining what authority and credentials they have on the matter in which it will be not much! You need to have the mindset that the only naysayers who want to give free and unrequested advice are the people who know nothing about what they are talking about and have nothing better to do!

As an example, the first editor who looked at my book Think and Be Rich and the Portal to Financial Gold told me that my book was shady and that I was just trying to scam people out of their money by writing it. I did not take her criticism kindly but then I asked myself, who is this person to make such ill claims against me and my book? I had realized that for one her degree was in creative writing and two she was just a writer and editor, but she did not have any degrees in that subject matter be it business or personal finance. She also did not have any experience to give such negative feedback regarding my book. Furthermore, she had sent a sample edit back to me full of errors in her edits with a juvenile and unprofessional suggested sentence that said "bilking more and more" when referring to companies gouging consumers, and so my conclusion was that she was not someone worthy of listening to in her criticism toward me. Now the point of this is not to just slam someone down but to get a point across that benefits my readers that you need to not listen to vicious and ill criticism and move forward with your goals and accomplishments. I will admit, however, that it is actually quite fun to retroactively tear this editor down in two of my books now, but I guess that is what she gets for her scathing criticism for no reason other than to tear me down in which I did not let it stop me at all to write a number one bestseller (declaration).

Additionally, you need to not let rejection stop you just because one person or one hundred people reject you. All of my closest friends and family rejected all of my business enterprises before I became successful. Everyone in my life including my blood family and my romantic partners became my number one critics in regards to my ability to be successful. I have heard it all: you won't be successful, you will never be self employed, you will never have a business, that's a terrible idea, you won't make any money doing that, no one is going to like what you have to offer, who would listen to you, and of course, you will never be rich. You need to keep moving forward even if everyone and I mean everyone and their mother tears you down, because guess what, everyone is going to tear you down. Only one percent of the entire population is rich and that means billions of people are going to tell you that you are never going to be successful in your endeavors.

When you continue to move forward with your endeavor, you will break through brick walls! Put your ego aside and DO NOT CARE what people think about you because it DOESN'T MEAN ANYTHING! And get new friends, those who will lift and support you! You also have to remain strong against their negativity no matter how many times you fail in front of them. My family watched me as I failed every year for a decade with every enterprise that I kept trying. Did I care? A BIG FAT NO! I didn't care if they felt like I was going to fail with this enterprise either because I knew that I would succeed with or without their approval. You need to not be discouraged by anyone especially your family and you also need to not let one hundred failures embarrass you. Now those who learn not to listen to other people's limitations for them in what they can and cannot do also learn to do what no one else will as we now go over in the next chapter.

Eli Scott |

Wealth Principle 4

Do what no one else will

If you want something you have never had, you must be willing to do something you have never done. -Thomas Jefferson

So now that we have gotten down not listening to others and that you too can be wealthy, we can go over one of the most important principles that you must follow if you want to become rich, and that is- doing what no one else will. If you are willing to do what no one else does, then you will massively increase your chances of becoming wealthy.

And so what must you be willing to do that no one else will? What rich people do that poor people don't is that they go to the extreme in making their wealth accumulate by cutting everything out in their lives that won't make them rich and staying laser focused on only the things that will. This means that you cut out everything in your life to having no life at all if that is what it takes to be wealthy and to not buy the things that other people do until you are wealthy.

So what does this look like?

I told you that this book is not for everyone in the introduction of this book, and if you didn't read the introduction, then here is another chance to understand that becoming massively wealthy is not for everyone because rich people have to do things a lot differently than what most people would find to be acceptable to do in order to get there. So to go to the extreme with this means to do the exact opposite of everything that poor people do. Poor people buy furniture and all the amenities of home first in order to be comfortable and to have an inviting home for their friends and family and then figure out how to pay for it later. Rich people work first to bring in millions of dollars and then buy the things that no one else can later.

Now you're probably saying, yeah right, I can still do those things, all of the normal things in life that everyone else does and still become rich someday, right? Wrong. Take it from a wealthy person who had to do those things from rags in order to become rich and I will tell you right now that every single one of these things is vitally important to your wealthfolio. Why? Because doing all of these things can mean the entire difference between whether you will have enough money to put a minimum of fifty to one hundred thousand dollars into a high net worth accredited private investment* that can make you well off someday and second, ignoring all of these distractions and working your butt off can be the difference of aspiring at the things that will make you wealthy. This might be the opposite of what society and everyone in your life want to tell you on what you should do in finding balance in your life in order to be happy and healthy like them, but these are the people who are not wealthy.

If you want to do what normal people do and what everyone else does who are not millionaires in their pursuits then you will have a normal life not made of money. Rich people on the other hand do not live the way poor people do or do the same things that poor people do. If they did, they would be poor! So if you want to be rich, you have to think like the rich and not have the same lifestyle that poor people do and giving up the comforts of life now in order to become rich later. Furthermore, you can't let your values be influenced by others around you- by how your friends and family, neighbors and coworkers spend their money or live the way they do.

While you may think that I'm full of horse poop on this, I can point out all of the wealthy people and I guarantee you that they don't get distracted by the things that normal people do in their everyday lives in order to become wealthy be it cleaning house, routine chores, cooking, recreation, hobbies, dating, family events, concerts, vacations, movies, TV, sports, news, and politics. It has been reported that there are many millionaires who are so busy running their money making enterprises that they don't even have time to eat like a normal person in which they stuff bites in whenever they can. I'm not saying that you have to go this extreme in your wealthy pursuits just yet, but what I am saying is that wealthy people do whatever it takes to become wealthy and that includes not living like that of a normal person in which they don't have time for anything else. You can go ahead and say screw that, there's no way I'm going to change my life to that extent and that is fine, but wealthy people live differently and it doesn't look anything like the lifestyle you are accustomed to that your poor community of family, friends, neighbors and teachers taught you. No self made millionaire carries that of a normal lifestyle and I didn't become successful in all of my endeavors in real estate, retirement plans, savings, my private investments, and my digital franchise by getting distracted with any of these things. You can laugh at me all you want but we are the ones who have the wealthy lifestyle that you only dream of.

Furthermore, you have to not only give up the comfortable and "normal" lifestyle that other people are used to, but you also have to once again not care what anyone thinks about you in the process, even if you lose all of your friends around you. As I said before who cares? They aren't the ones who are making you rich, and you will make new friends in the process, those of other wealthy people who will serve you in supporting your new lifestyle. Additionally, those who are serious in going this extreme to become wealthy won't care how uncomfortable, lonely, or deprived they are because they know they are doing the things that will make them wealthy and not doing the things that creates a mediocre or broke lifestyle.

Also know that you won't have to be this extreme in your sacrifices for your entire life, but those who are serious will do this for as long as it takes to get wealthy. Do I have more leisure today? Yes, but it wasn't until I worked my butt off to see my potential fortune that I allowed myself to have a normal life. Once you have boosted your business or money-making success, then you can have time for your husband or your wife, for children and family, and television and video games. I also know it can be very difficult to cut things out of your life in which I suggest to try cutting out hobbies, recreation, leisure, and other activities for a few nights as you focus on doing things that can make you wealthy. Eventually, you will start finding yourself to do this for weeks, months, and even years if you are dead serious on becoming wealthy.

Do what no one else will also means to DO the things that no one else will in manifesting your wealth for you in trekking your own destiny and doing unique things in founding your own business or tech company, creating your own albums, to starting your own production companies, running your own successful business, seeking alternative private investments, or in my case, writing my own books under my own publishing company. When you struggle to become employed at what it is that can make you wealthy, you simply go outside the norm of what anyone else is doing and do the opposite of what everyone else is to go your own way in amassing wealth to you.

Now with all of that being said, I am not suggesting that anyone cut out their work out programs or exercise routines as there are many people namely athletes who have to work out and build muscle in order to become massively wealthy. Exercise can also help build discipline, boost your energy, and bring fresh thoughts and ideas to boost your wealth making opportunities to you. You also might have noticed that I didn't say to not buy a house. You should certainly buy a house if you are up against steep apartment rental prices and or you feel you can make a good profit on it in rental income or by flipping it. You should not buy a house if it's outside of your means to do so or can turn you upside down from the market. As a disclaimer to this, it is advisable to always speak to a lawyer before buying any real estate or property. Also watch out for high HOA fees which can literally destroy you.

I am also not saying that you should be a coupon clipper as that takes up precious time needed to stay laser focused on the things that will make you wealthy and every moment is critical as we will go over in another chapter. Although there are rich people who do clip coupons, this doesn't mean you should when you don't know how this time-consuming task can interfere with your upcoming success in which you should consider waiting until you have more time for this task once you have become wealthy. There are many other less time-consuming ways you can be thrifty in bargain shopping for cheap cars, phones, clothes, and furniture, some of which you can buy at thrift stores or second hand in the case of furniture from trusted family to avoid bug infestation like many rich and famous people do. There are also many millionaires who live in small duplexes, condos, townhomes and even trailer homes while driving the same car that they have for the past twenty years as they build their wealth to them.

Doing what it takes to become wealthy involves making steep sacrifices and then working through the grueling pain of what it takes to get there. If you are one of the few who is willing to go to this extreme to become massively rich and wealthy, then I invite you to the next wealth principle in taking action and doing in order to receive which we now go over in the next chapter.

*There is no guarantee of results in any investment. Additionally, high net worth accredited and private investments can be highly risky. If you want to work with any of these types of investments, it would be of benefit to you to not do so without seeking legal advice and working with qualified licensed brokers to help you. There are qualifications you must meet to become an accredited investor. The accredited investor requirements can be located through **https://www.sec.gov**.

Eli Scott |

Wealth Principle 5

———————————

You must do to receive

Success is not something to wait for, it is something to work for.
-Henry Wadsworth Longfellow

Our greatest weakness lies in giving up. The most certain way to succeed is always to try just one more time.
-Thomas A. Edison

Give me six hours to cut down a tree and I will spend the first four sharpening the axe.
-Abraham Lincoln

When it comes to doing what it takes to become wealthy, you must do! Becoming rich is not about buying into fairy tales of those who simply become rich out of no where, but by doing what it really takes, what is REAL in making millions of dollars for you. In order to show what is and isn't real in becoming wealthy, I will start with one concept that has exploded in the last fifty or so years in that of using the law of attraction to bring fortune to you. What most law of attraction principles tout is that you can get rich by simply wishing for it or by being positive in attracting wealth to you. The law of attraction, however, does not work that way. There is not some sort of magical phenomenon that will reward you with money just because you ask for it. Additionally, the time and energy it takes to become rich is not about turning your negative mindset into that of a positive one in attracting wealth to you or even paying into a bunch of programs and systems that you think will make you rich. If any of these things could make anyone rich then my goodness we would all be rich! While all of these things can be helpful in bringing money to you, where the law of attraction comes into play for your millionaire success is rather a) getting back what you give to others and b) getting back what value you put into the market and working your butt off to get there. So if you are not already wealthy, do not think that you can pray to your ceiling or wish upon a star every night that a vault of money will come to you.

As a case in point, I remember following the law of attraction principles written in a book I read in which I declared my positive mental vibes to the deities above in my wish to become rich and I literally heard the words "you need to get off your butt and work for it!" being blasted back at me through my ceiling from this mystical invisible force from above. What this meant to me was that my wishing was useless without doing. So when resorting to the law of attraction to make you rich and wealthy, it comes down to what you put into it and the massive action that you take every day to build your wealth for you because it doesn't come to bums who stand on the corner with their signs everyday simply asking for it while not doing anything for it.

So now what do I mean by massive action? Taking massive action means doing whatever it takes until one day you finally see your wealth explode for you. If you have read any of my other books, you probably know that I like to use acronyms. One key acronym that I use in Think and Be Rich and the Portal to Financial Gold is to gain personal wealth by working your A-S-S off. While this acronym stands for assets, savings, and spending in that book, in this book it represents that of becoming wealthy through your:

A – Action

S - Study and

S – Sweat

You have to work and hustle with your action, study, and sweat if you want to be wealthy. However, as you can tell by the words in this acronym, it's not going to be easy and you must work non stop even when you don't know where your endeavors are going to get you or what return you will get on them. But if you want it that bad then you have to be willing to do anything and I mean anything every second of every day of your life with the stubborn mindset that you will be rich and it will be one of the hardest things you will ever do in your life as you go through the severe pain in amassing wealth to you. Working your A-S-S off through the PAIN holds the secret formula in achieving the most success for you. So what type of pain do I speak of?

When I speak of pain, I mean really struggling through the difficulties and challenges ahead of you. Doing what it takes to become wealthy will put you through a lot of physical, mental, and emotional anguish and irritation (the

A and I in pain) as you work through your challenges and obstacles to your success. You will also be under a lot of pressure and up against a lot of negativity (the P and N in pain) in what you can and cannot do. However, if you are willing to work hard through the severe pain everyday then you can attract your mountainous treasure in gaining your biggest asset for you. An asset is something that you own or have that is either worth a lot of money or can make you a lot of money. Your biggest asset is what will bring the most wealth to you and is best summed up in the following Think and Be Rich formula:

Your Biggest Asset = ((Education + Hustle + Cash Flow (savings and income) – Debt) ^ Time = Wealth Accumulation

Now don't worry as you don't have to figure out what this formula means because I will simply explain it to you. Your biggest asset is the combination of your education, hard work, and cash flow (money coming into your bank account), minus all of your debt, multiplied by the power of time which will determine your total wealth accumulation ahead of you. While part of this equation has to do with your own personal financial management, a huge portion of gaining wealth is by the time and energy it takes for you to accumulate your wealth by receiving the knowledge and skills that allow you to work at careers and money making opportunities that pay a lot of money to you. While some people find success in things that don't require degrees, those who find the most success are those who work hard in anything that they do. Just as Abraham Lincoln said, it takes more time to sharpen the blade than it does to achieve your end goal.

So rather than thinking of the pain itself, think of the pain bringing a wealth of prosperity, affluence or abundance, income, and your nest egg of high net worth to you. That is, going through the pain (Pressure, Anguish, Irritation, and Negativity) that you can then turn into PAIN

Turn PAIN into PAIN

From > To

Pressure to Prosperity

Anguish to Abundance

Irritation to Income

Negativity to Nest egg of high net worth

Those who do to receive also make every moment critical in arousing their fortune and they once again take this to the extreme. What rich people do that poor people don't is that they severely leverage their time as everything they do is the exact difference of whether they will be rich someday. What does that mean? It means they don't waste any time. You need to have the mindset that every second of every day and everything you do to make your dreams a reality for you is critical in your success to achieve your wealth for you. And so do I think I would be where I'm at today if I had not followed this wealth principle to the extreme? Absolutely not, because everything I did took a lot of time and effort in which I would be broke if didn't hustle every second of it.*

Furthermore, I wouldn't be where I'm at today without my entire history to stay focused to learn the ins and outs of business and entrepreneurship. So this is the same mindset that you need to carry is that every waking moment is critical in amassing your fortune to you and no self made millionaire does it without working sun up to sun down seven days a week sometimes in order to continue running their business or doing whatever it is that they do to bring massive fortune to them.

Along with that, you need to follow the wealth principle to keep moving, that is, keep working at it every day even if you are only getting a little bit done each day. As many people throughout time have said, if you can't run then walk and what matters is that you do not stop. With constant progress, no matter how little, you will eventually build your enterprise for you.

Now the law of attraction also works in other ways, other than just working for it to bring wealth to you. The law of attraction also works on the level of the thoughts, beliefs, and can do attitude that you too can be wealthy against all odds for you as we will go over in another chapter.

For now, we need to get down the grueling work it takes to become that multi-millionaire which brings us to finding your motivation to work through the pain by being painfully desperate for it as we discuss in the next wealth principle ahead.

*In the process of making every moment critical for you, I am not suggesting that you be negligent to yourself or others around you who you are obligated to. Those who become wealthy use every critical moment that they can but still tend to their vital matters or hire help for their vital matters if they can.

Eli Scott |

Wealth Principle 6

You must be painfully desperate for it

If you want to make life easy, make it hard. -Johann Wolfgang von Goethe

So now as I was saying in the last wealth principle, you must take action and do in order to receive a lot of wealth to you. Yet, it is so easy for us all to come home every single day with excuses to not do as we laze on the couch doing anything but working hard for it. So why is it that we can't seem to find the motivation to get off our butts and do? It all comes down to how badly you want it. It does not at all matter how much money a get rich system promises to make you, no amount of money moves anyone to pursue past their laziness or lack of reason in doing. Therefore, you have to find what will motivate you to work through the pain and the only way you can do that is to be in more pain than the pain it will take to enterprise you. You must be in enough pain and suffering before you will suffer even more which pushes you that much further.

So now how can we get ourselves to be in that much pain? The first thing you need to do is to not be comfortable with your lifestyle as we went over in wealth principle four. If all of your needs are met and you are not desperate for money, then you will not be motivated but rather numbed and paralyzed to do anything in life beyond what you are already doing. I have everything I need, therefore, I don't need to pursue money for the sake of money. So while money in itself is not a motivator for becoming rich, being too comfortable can also stifle your desire to do the things that will make you rich.

While there are many ways that we can ensure we are not too comfortable, one of the biggest things that can help us be so is in that of a lack of money. Throughout my Think and Be Rich book series, I chose to leave out my misfortune in losing a lot of money throughout my lifetime because I didn't want to sound whiney. But I do find an appropriate reason to mention it here and that is, I was not personally motivated to work my butt off every single day to do what it took in order to become massively wealthy until I lost out on an entire lifetime of savings, say one hundred thousand dollars in medical bills and stupid debt. Why would that motivate me? By losing so much hard earned money over my lifetime, I became very angry with all of my potential investment and real estate opportunities that could have made me that much more wealthy. Furthermore, I was even more angry at how much time and work it took to make that money, to work so hard for so little every day over a twenty year span and to have nothing to show for it. This extreme anger was what allowed me to find my reason, my WHY that pushed me to learn how to leverage my money.

What really motivated me to work my butt off even more in my wealth path was when two things happened: One, I was working for only twenty nine thousand dollars a year a at an hourly job when my boss decided to cut my hours to give to a new hire, and two, I had a horrible boss at another job who lied on my performance review for three years in a row in order to steal approximately fifteen thousand dollars in bonus money from me. Both of these things allowed me to use my anger from this in my favor to motivate me to work that much harder at the things that would make me wealthy. Instead of fighting for my rightful hours back, I decided to use the time to pursue my other money making opportunities which would help me to quit that job that much faster!

So now you have to find your severe motivation to become wealthy and that may not happen until you are angry or in enough pain whether it's steep debt to seeing the looks in your children's faces when you can't get them that new bicycle or whatever it is they want, to not being able to pay your rent, or the money you have lost throughout your lifetime that you will then be willing to work even harder to get it all back to you in a shorter amount of time. Along with that, you should also see the blessing in disguise of losing a lot of money in your favor, because it will again be the pain created by that that will push you to work ten times harder to amass wealth to you.

If you can't find your reason or pain in financial loss, then you can find other things that can motivate you. Some of the other things that motivated me to become wealthy is that I don't have to get up every morning and go slave at a job that I hate, I don't have to sit in long lines of traffic to get to and from work everyday, I don't have to give into exploitation at a job, and I can go anywhere in the world that I want to at any time. I have time freedom, I have money freedom, I have travel freedom. But even more significant than any of these things is that I don't have to be in any more pain and suffering as I struggle to pay the bills everyday.

Being painfully desperate for it also means potentially risking your financial future by not increasing your skillsets in any jobs that will not make you wealthy so that you can focus on the enterprises that will. This method, however, is only for those who know for absolute sure that they will succeed at something and can do so without jeopardizing their future. In order to focus on my wealthy endeavors, I intentionally stayed at the bottom of the chain at all of my jobs and ignored increasing my skillsets at a traditional job so that I could increase my skillsets on the ambitions that would make me wealthy. In the process, I was very uncomfortable and I knew that my life was at stake which kept me motivated to work hard at my wealthy endeavor that would secure my financial future. However, I stayed employed at many jobs and made profits in real estate while working hard at my wealth path to have some sort of a safety net for my future.

Now being painfully desperate does not mean to be desperate with your money and what you do with it. Those who get rich don't give into financial investments and policies that will only financially destroy them but to leverage your money with the right types of financial investments, careers, vocations, or other wealth enterprises that will work for you and not against you as we will go over more in wealth principle thirteen. Being painfully desperate for it is about what will motivate you to work through the grueling pain to accomplish by finding your passion and reason to do as well as finding yourself in doing it as we discuss in the next chapter.

Eli Scott |

Wealth Principle 7

You must find yourself in doing it

The writer must earn money in order to be able to live and to write, but he must by no means live and write for the purpose of making money. -Karl Marx

Now this is the shortest chapter in this book, but being that this is simply a guidebook on lifestyles and attitudes in becoming wealthy, I can break the rules a little bit. I also could not combine this wealth principle with another and is one of the most important wealth principles that needs to discussed before the rest of the others. We will also expand upon this principle in the rest of the chapters. So with that all being said I don't think you will really care how short this chapter is as it provides a powerful formula in becoming wealthy and that is you must find yourself in doing it. By that, I mean that you must find your passion and reason to do as well as how your life will fit into it. Why is this important? Because you will not have the severe drive that it takes to become wealthy until you have found these things.

As science has proven, we all naturally need certain things in our lives from having all of our basic needs met in that of our survival but also that of love in romantic partners and friends and family around us as well as purpose before we can focus on the things, the enterprises that will make us massively wealthy. As stupid and trivial as these things sound, it has been known many times over that even the most successful and wealthy people can and have failed at their wealthy endeavors by not having these things. As a case in point, I have talked to lawyers and doctors and have heard of prominent venture capitalists who have all left their careers because they were unhappy and unfulfilled in which they took pay cuts in order to find all of these things. It is also known by universities that even college students chose their majors based on the social aspects of how their love life and family will fit into it and the values they carry in pursuing their studies. Furthermore, I did not find my motivation to pursue the things that promised to make me massively wealthy when I couldn't find my why or see how my life was going to fit into it.

So if you want me to cut ten to fifteen years down from the time it will take for you to become wealthy, then I highly suggest you pay attention to this wealth principle in bringing fortune to you. You can fail at any enterprise when your only incentive is to make a lot of money when you can't find your life and your heart in it. It is as Karl Marx says that you must not do for the sake of money. Replace the writer in this quote with any profession and see that you are never moved by the money. If you are not fulfilled by it or don't care about it and can't find how your lifestyle will fit into it, then you will be one of the people who lets all of these ambitions pile up in the corner of your room as you sit around to not make anything happen with any of them. You need to find what your values are if you are trying to become explosively successful with any enterprise. Once you figure out your reason to do, then you will work eighty hours a week to enterprise you.

I will give pursuing real estate as an example. Why real estate? Because it seems to be the most highly touted get rich system in which I ask, if real estate is that easy and can make anyone rich, then why aren't we all going into real estate to become rich and more importantly, why aren't we all getting rich with it? While some can find success with it, there are really two reasons it doesn't make everyone wealthy and that is for one you are heavily relying on the markets in which it can be risky and does in fact cause even the wealthiest people to lose a lot of money and two, it takes a lot of grueling hustle in which you have to find your drive in doing it. Now I know there will be readers here who will say that real estate really isn't that hard especially when you can automate it, meaning to buy into a bunch of systems that will take a lot of the hefty work off of you. My response to this is that real estate gets a lot more complicated than that when there are too many strategies in which not one single one guarantees results and even seasoned real estate gurus have to constantly strategize in a constantly changing market. Not everyone has the desire to hustle real estate when they don't know how their life will fit into it and what their values are in doing it.

So now how do we find our passion and reason to do? This is a question that comes with a very complicated answer but the first suggestion I can give is to find your true self first. And how do we do that? We start by not listening to others and by listening to ourselves. You inherently know what it is that you love and what your burning passion is when you wake up every morning or take that refreshing afternoon walk. You are also naturally moved by what matters to you and will do when your heart and burning passion collide with your ambitions. You also know when to not do when you can't force yourself in doing it. Simply put, you just do or don't. However, finding your passion and why can get much deeper than this in which there are other things we can do to find our passion. While we will go over other ways to find yourself and your why in other wealth principles ahead, one very powerful thing you can do is to narrow your options and to detoxify and get rid of anyone and anything that is not serving you as we go over in the next chapter.

Eli Scott |

Wealth Principle 8

Get rid of anyone and anything not serving you

All you need in this life is ignorance and confidence, and then success is sure. -Mark Twain

In wealth principle number five, I seem to claim that the law of attraction doesn't exist. However, the law of attraction does exist, just not in the way that a lot of books tout. While you can't just wish and you shall have, the law of attraction exists on many levels to bring fortune to you in that of your mindset as well as what we tolerate and accept that shapes and molds how you will act and what you will do in attracting your environment and wealth to you.

Whatever positive or negative energy you tolerate and accept is what will be brought back to you. So you can use the law of attraction to attract wealth to come to you in that you don't accept or tolerate any negativity or toxins from other people or your environment around you. I know this seems to contradict what I said before in that a positive mindset doesn't bring wealth to you, however, you can't attract wealth if you don't do and you let others discourage you. It is with all of this then that the law of attraction works by saying no to what you don't want, saying yes to what you do want, and then enforcing it. You enforce what it is you do or do not want by cutting everything out of your life that isn't going to get you there and then taking action. This now brings us to wealth principle eight which is to detoxify your life in order to set up the stage to attract wealth to you.

It will be on you to make the decisions and take the actions to release and get rid of everything that is holding you back from achieving your abundance and success be it the home that you do not want to live in, the enterprise you do not want to pursue, and toxic relationships in your life. Now I'm not telling you to quit your job, divorce your spouse, or sell your house if you are not in a position to do so, however, the most successful people are not held down by anything, be it a career or a house or a spouse. Your life path is yours and you only allow those in your life who will uplift you in your ambitions to get there. So to detoxify your life is to detox or get rid of anyone in your life not serving you and holding you down whether it's your parents, your significant others, your friends and family, your neighbors and teachers, and yes even your husband or wife if you are able to do so. If you can't get rid of a spouse (or don't want to leave them) then find a way to work around them regardless of their attitude towards you. Have a zero tolerance policy to the people in your life who only hold you down and don't serve you in the way you need to be to get you there.

At one point I had nothing against dating low wage workers until two things happened: one, they started asking me to pay their bills and two, they became downers to any of my career aspirations. I am not intending to just bad mouth low wage workers and I am also not saying that you are like this just because you are a low wage worker. I would say that about ten percent of low wage workers have the right mentally and if you are one of the few reading this then you have the positive no non-sense attitude to lift up yourself and others in becoming wealthy. But back to my story of low wage workers, all of the ones I dated were toxic in their extreme arrogance that they think they know everything in telling me what I could and couldn't do. Furthermore, they lack the ambition and right attitude in which they are not in the least successful. Therefore, I chose to ignore and exclude them from my life in order to succeed at the things that will make me wealthy and I certainly don't need any downers to stop my along the way.

As an example, I dated a twenty seven year old back in 2011 who was making thirty thousand dollars a year and living with his parents in their trailer home who told me that I was not going to succeed in life with my wealthy ambitions. I told him that my train was leaving with or without him, meaning I was going to aspire at my dreams whether he approved or not and that I was going to leave him behind. While I personally encourage anyone to live with their parents and in trailer homes especially in our current economy, I certainly wasn't going to listen to someone who didn't know anything about what it takes to become wealthy first and foremost and that is your attitude that you will and then having the discipline to work at it every day.

Along with not tolerating toxic relationships or people, it's important that you don't buy their excuses either. I once posted an eviction notice on a roommate's bedroom door (who was renting out a room in my home) for not abiding by my house rules. While I'm going to spare you the details of how overly gross this man was, because yes he was *that* gross, I didn't buy any excuses from a very disgusting person who couldn't respect me and my needs to have a clean house. If you want to attract likable and ideal romantic partners and people in your life, then only accept relationships with those types of people. That is how the law of attraction works.

On the flip side of that, you need to be what you seek. If you want a good spouse who treats you right, you need to be the person who is worthy in what you can offer first because someone who has a lot to offer is only going to look for the person who has a lot to offer. With that being said, if you want a clean house, you need to be clean. If you want a person with a good attitude, you need to have a good attitude. If you want someone who is loving and caring, you need to be loving and caring. And if you want to be rich and attract a rich or well off person then you need to have those same qualities that you can offer. Along with all of that, people are more willing to support you and buy from you when you are yourself giving and appreciative of them. I myself will only help and buy from people who are more giving and appreciative of me.

Detoxifying also means to get rid of anything at all that could keep you from moving forward be it the ten thousand pounds of junk in your home, physical possessions, various memberships and subscriptions, unnecessary obligations, a million things distracting you, and limited beliefs in enterprising you. What does junk and clutter have to do with anything? We can't think clearly when our house is cluttered because it makes us think too much about those things even when they are out of sight. These are things we tend to put on the back burner which can physically block your concentration and focus when you know they are sitting around somewhere. These things can also bog you down and create obstacles that take our time and attention away from doing things that will bring our fortune.

Now once again you're probably saying yeah right... these things don't matter in becoming wealthy and I will tell you right now as a true rags to riches story that cutting all of these things out of your life critically matter in becoming wealthy. Why? Because you need to stay laser focused on the one thing that will make you rich and these things weigh you down and distract you from doing the things that will enterprise you. Rich people don't let these things block them and instead throw everything out including ten different get rich systems so that they can stay laser focused on the one thing that will make them wealthy.

So if you have ten different get rich systems, side hustles*, or business ideas piling up in the corner of your bedroom, I guarantee you will not find fortune in any of them. Examples of these many different ambitions could be starting your own ecommerce store, commercial real estate, foreign exchange or day trading, bitcoin and cryptocurrencies, multi level marketing programs, supplemental health insurance programs, and starting clothing lines or tech apps in which your head swells and dwells in the what ifs in becoming rich in any of them while they sit around as you do nothing with them. If you haven't pursued them by now that you aren't going to in ten years from now either and you can only focus on one thing to become successful in which you throw the rest out. Additionally, those who get rich are the ones who also don't have any limiting beliefs as to who they can be and what they can do. They learn how to power through and again just do through the challenges of it all. They also run faster from the toxic people who discourage them and set their limitations for them. However, we will go over finding your inner strength and battling through your own limiting beliefs in another chapter.

Before we end here, I want to go over letting go of unnecessary obligations a little bit further. You have probably guessed by now that these things include events and hobbies and what not but being that I'm the extreme queen, I will tell you that this also includes careers that won't serve you. Although we need our jobs in order to make a living, we can still find ourselves becoming too dependent on them in which we feel obligated to them. I came upon this revelation that my job was holding me back in my pursuits when I was meditating one day on what it would take to become wealthy in which the first answer I got back from above was to let everything go that was holding me back including my house, my belongings, and even my employer! It was at that very moment that I realized I had this mindset that I felt obligated to my employer that I *had* to work for them, that I actually had to stay there every single day for the rest of my life because I owed it to them. This was an eye opening discovery for me that many people, the general public at large has the same thought that they are in debt to their employer and that they are obligated to serve them for the rest of their lives. Even if they don't feel this way, they at least feel as though they are stuck there because they can't do anything else and chances are, you are one or both of these people! So if you feel stuck at a job that you feel of holding back, one of the things you have to do is realize that you are not in fact obligated to your employer, you don't owe them anything, and you do have options to get out of it and to be wealthy if you have what it takes to get there. You need to have the stubborn can-do attitude and be above normalcy in achieving wealth to you and do as rich people do in letting go of that ball and chain job that won't make you wealthy and only focus on the things that will.

One final note is that the quote in the beginning of this chapter is not meaning to say that you should be ignorant, but to simply ignore distractions and toxic people and confidently do to bring your fortune to you.

Now those who will find the most success are those who learn to run from any of these people or these things and to accomplish their goals and desires faster. The best way to accomplish this is to simplify and that's what we will go over in the next wealth principle ahead.

*I am not discouraging you from having a side hustle that actually pays you as this is a means of building important savings that you can then put towards lucrative investments for you. I am only stating to run faster from those side hustles you are not pursuing or not serving you. It's important to go for the side hurdles that pay you guaranteed wages, tips or commissions without your up front investments and no guarantee of any payments.

Eli Scott |

Wealth Principle 9

Simple sells and simplify

Truth is ever to be found in simplicity, and not in the multiplicity and confusion of things. -Isaac Newton

The person attempting to travel two roads at once will get nowhere. -Xunzi

Even though I prefaced this chapter with the last in simplifying what you do to bring wealth to you, simplifying really has many functionalities in business and success all of which we will discuss in this chapter. Simplifying can mean anything from doing things easier to narrowing your goals to how you tackle problems and even to what you sell.

It has been known that some of the most successful businesses have done very well by being very simple in what they sell- only having a few items on the food menu as opposed to thirty at restaurants, only selling a few types of eyeglasses, or only selling one item. The same simplicity is true for websites and writing materials. The most successful websites and books are very simple in that they are black on white with very few images and very little color on them. Additionally, the number one selling book in the world is written in plain English, meaning that it doesn't have any difficult vocab in it. So why is it that simplicity sells better with all of these various things?

Simple is a lot easier on the brain and can keep people's attention much longer. Customers tend to become confused and overwhelmed when they have too many items to chose from when it comes to catalogs, stores, product lines, and restaurant menus. Overwhelm and confusion in what you have to offer many times leads to customers abandoning the sale altogether. The same can happen when there's too many images with color on websites. Research has shown that black on white and few images is just plain simpler which sells better than too many images with color which tend to clutter and overwhelm people. Simple written books are also a lot easier to read and understand and therefore attract the largest amount of readers and therefore make the most sales.

It is known and taught by many schools, institutions, and other organizations that dumbing down anything is of upmost importance in any type of writing, educational, or instructional material. Not to sound too cliché but the most overused phrase for this is keep it simple stupid or keep it simple silly, also known as KISS. Dumbing down is the most important thing to do in order to get the most people to understand you and is also the biggest objective of technical writing courses. Technical writing is not about making writing more technical and difficult, but how to make it less so by using the simplest to understand vocab and writing. By dumbing it down, people can understand and absorb the reading better. You may have also noticed that although my books are about personal finance, I don't put any math in any of them. Why? Because first of all I absolutely hate math and want nothing to do with it but also because I can reach a much bigger audience by simply not including it in any of my writing materials.

Moving onto narrowing goals, the wealthiest people will focus on one and only one thing that will make them wealthy, which now coincides with the last chapter. Of course you can argue with me if you want to, but let me ask you if you are someone who is either successful or has ten "get rich" systems collecting dust in the corner of your bedroom (or in the back of your mind). The problem with trying to become successful by aspiring in ten enterprises is that your attention gets divided ten different ways and none of them will succeed when you are only putting one fifth of your attention, time and energy into it. And even if all of your get rich systems and ideas are just piled up in your house somewhere, you can still be distracted by the what if's in any one of them making you wealthy. In other words, they take up precious room in your head as you dwell on them.

All of your time and attention is needed for one thing to make it successful and don't think you can try to be successful with five or six companies by putting more work onto your employees. There are notable cases of multi billionaires losing lots of money (tens of billions of dollars) when they didn't focus on trying to make one thing successful and thought they could just exhaust their employees by telling them to work harder and longer. This has led to massive resignations at big name companies and the resulting crash of some billionaire's fortunes. Therefore, one of the first things you want to do is to narrow your goal to one path that will lead you to massive success.

Simplifying also means that you too can become wealthy by looking for opportunity in the simplest places. As an example, I found it too difficult to try to become wealthy by being the next tech giant as that requires a lot of engineering and marketing to launch those kinds of enterprises. After my many years of failed attempts of discovering the next big invention, I found a simple opportunity to rewrite in the personal finance genre by filling in gaps I saw in other books. You too may chose to not go after such big ambitions that can create too many personal challenges and instead look for opportunity in all of the small and not so obvious places. The only thing to keep in mind with this tactic, however, is that you have to keep your eyes wide open in looking for hidden gems and know that it can take time before you may find any.

Simplifying also means to not get bogged down in information overload. When it comes to becoming wealthy, the most disastrous thing you can do is let an entire library of books fall onto you. Those who simply get rich don't waste a lot of time and just do it. They don't try to become a walking encyclopedia by learning information or everything there is to know about a product. Those who do will find themselves going down the rabbit hole of destruction as they never move forward in their business. A successful entrepreneur will simply get to work while having resources that they can refer to rather than trying to memorize everything.

This now brings me to the quick tale of the mystical jellyfish. This was a tale that was originally meant to be in my book Think and be Rich and The Portal to Financial Gold, but I didn't find it appealing to include in that book in which I do find an appropriate spot for it here. The tale of the mystical jellyfish begins in that of a jellyfish that you see mindlessly floating in the distance ahead of you in which I let him tell you his story:

"As you see in this mystical night sky, I am simply gliding by. It is with my clear body and effortless do, that I scry the following things onto you: As you dive into these misty seas, you will start to arouse transparencies, and as you go on your venture to build your crew, you will simply let the sun shine through. It is in these ray of lights that I am able to penetrate many sights.

As you continue on your journey, everything will begin to speak to you. When you tread ten thousand miles, you will be able to effortlessly spew. The tale of those who simply get rich are not about those who get buried under information overload but to glide through it to our destiny. It is not the ten thousand pounds of books or knowledge that you need but simply that of letting the information of what is already here bleed."

So what does this poem mean? In simple words, it means to stop getting bogged down in information because the information is already here. All you have to do is reference it. And as you continue to practice and do, everything will effortlessly come to you. You also don't need to get weighed down in the rigors of school and to rise above it to your destiny. Now, I'm not saying school isn't important. School is important as I go over in the another chapter, but for now, we are only talking about simplicity in manifesting wealth to you. Which reminds me that even laziness in itself has created some of the wealthiest people. I work hard at my wealthy endeavors so that that I can retire from a slave job at the age of forty.

On a side note, you don't have to be an early riser to be wealthy as some wealthy people like to preach to the contrary. What is the difference between an early riser who gets to work at five am, and someone who works until three am? There is no difference if you both are putting in the work that it takes to become wealthy, and this is really what being an early riser to be rich is really about is putting in the hours. Additionally, some of the most successful people build passive income where they can earn money in their sleep! The people who need to be early risers are those who work for corporations or have to speak to other people in the early morning hours, but otherwise, you can "sleep in" as much as you want to. When I say sleep in, I don't mean that in the way of someone who goes to bed early and then wakes up late. By sleeping in, I'm talking about those who don't go to sleep until late and then wake up late.

There are a couple more things I must mention when it comes to simplifying and narrowing your business matters before I end here. At the same time that simple sells, you don't want to go too little in a business opportunity if you are looking to go big in your endeavors. What I mean by that is that there is still a difference between a huge commercial opportunity and a small one. You will know what I mean if you ever watch Shark Tank or Dragon's Den from various countries throughout the world which are amongst my favorite shows to watch. These Sharks and Dragons will not invest in businesses and ideas that are too small meaning they have too little and too niche (too specialized or too divisional) of a market. They will, however, invest in simple ideas and businesses that appeal to a much broader market. As examples for each, the Dragons in the United Kingdom wouldn't invest in a figure skater's idea to sell clothes and apparel that would only appeal to figure skaters because that is too little of a market, meaning that it would not appeal to the mass market. Big investors such as these will, however, invest in things that appeal to everyone and can bring in big business even if they are simple such as new social media apps and tech companies.

At the same time, these big investors will not invest in things that are so simple that too many other competitors can create them or the products are not needed at all. As an example, some of the UK Dragon's Den investors wouldn't invest in a board game when it was so simple to play that you could play it without the game at all. Others did invest in it when they were able to find ways to make the game a little more complicated. So there is a difference between simplifying and creating big business versus simplifying and going too small or too simple in manifesting wealth for you. If you can create a small business that does well in bringing income to you, however, then more power to you.

Finally, the most invention minded people are those who find ways to make lives easier and not harder for people and they become wealthy by simplifying and taking the easier routes in their own performance to get there. This now brings us to doing the opposite of what they teach you in school in the next wealth principle ahead.

Eli Scott |

Wealth Principle 10

Do the opposite of what they teach you in school

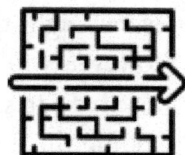

Life is really simple, but we insist on making it complicated.
-Confucius

Being simple and simplifying everything now brings us to this next wealth principle which is doing the opposite of what they teach you in school. I'm not talking about doing what no one else will here but in how to tackle your everyday projects and problems when it comes to your tasks and work in your wealth enterprises. This is best explained once again by what the rich do differently than the poor to amass their wealth to them. Poor people let themselves get tied up and weighed down by the rigors of challenging difficult problems. Rich people on the other hand do things as quick and as easy as possible to accomplish their goals for them. And so how is this the opposite of what they teach you in school?

Do you remember your eighth grade math teacher telling you to do the hardest and most difficult problems first and then work your way down to the easiest ones? I certainly do, and I remember thinking even in the eighth grade as this not being the best advice. I have learned this to be even more true now that I have found success in my endeavors and have taken project management courses through my college career. We won't get into project management too much here, but I will give my sage advice when it comes to working on business and projects by solving the easiest problems first through what I call the path of least resistance. With the path of least resistance, you will find that when you work on the easiest, tiniest, and fastest to resolve problems or tasks first that you find the most success for you.

When we tackle the hardest and most difficult problems first, they can be very stubborn and resistant against you and in some cases can become impossible to do. This also leads to exhaustion and discouragement for you.

Additionally, when we tackle the hardest problems first, they are capable of not ever get resolved leaving everything behind it to also remain unresolved. The best scenario I can give for this is to think of a bunch of cords all tied up in a knot. Sometimes when you try to unravel it from the center, the knot is so severely tight that you can't unravel it, leaving the entire knot to stay knotted. However, you may find yourself to work on the easier and less knotted and loosened parts first in which you find yourself unraveling the entire knot. So by tackling the easiest items first, you will find that the rest of the problems, no matter how difficult, tend to work themselves out.

To give a quick example using my book writing, I find some of the chapters in my drafts to be very difficult in which I get bogged down in trying to tackle them. Anytime my work gets too complicated or confusing, I always tell myself that it's meant to be easy. I then solve this challenge by simplifying it in which I tackled the easiest chapters first. By doing this, I many times come to realize that I don't need to include some of the hardest chapters at all and can just delete them out entirely. When you find yourself getting bogged down in difficult tasks everyday, you will end up wasting a lot of precious time which can completely destroy you in ever finding success to you. By following the path of least resistance, you will be able to trash anything not worthy of your time a lot faster in which you will explode your ambitions for you.

The same principle applies with your agenda and to-do list. Writing long and complicated to-do lists can become very overwhelming in which you may find yourself discouraged to do anything. Long to-do lists may involve difficult tasks and too many things that distract you. Additionally, a bunch of little tasks everyday serves no purpose other than to make you feel busy. The best thing to do is to never have more than three to five items on your to-do list daily, and to tackle the biggest thing that will bring you the most success everyday in which you will find all of the other little things to naturally take care of themselves in the process.

Now, I am going to put a small twist on this which is that you can still approach tasks and problems from both angles. In my projects, I can find myself going back and forth to tackle either the easier problems or the harder ones depending on what can't be avoided in solving and doing. Sometimes we just have to hit the nail on the head and that is perfectly fine too. The point is to know when to tackle things from an easier angle when the harder end is getting you no where or is just plain frustrating you. This is also known as being agile (meaning to adapt to plans by changing how you tackle the project) in which you can choose to tackle things from many angles depending on what you need to do.

In addition to tackling issues and projects from many angles, you can also do tasks in a variety of orders such as geometric or living order. These are two common orders of doing things in project management that were introduced by French philosopher Henri Bergson. Geometric order is where you follow a plan in chronological order (A to B to C) and is linear, predetermined and predictable, whereas living order is adaptable, creative, and flexible (tackling from any angle or order). To use my book writing as an example again, there are some successful book authors who have written books on how to be a successful book author in which they claim that you need to always tackle the book writing from a predetermined and chronological order by creating an outline of your book before you begin writing it as a way to give you a clear picture on what to write. They may also tell you to write the whole book in chronological order from the first chapter to the last (known as chronological or geometric order). In my book writing projects, I have found it to be beneficial to just start writing first before creating an outline, because sometimes I have a lot to write but don't always know what the outline should look like until I know what overall message I'm trying to get across to my readers. I also write chapters as they come to me in living order and not in chronological order, meaning I just start writing as my thoughts come to me and I organize them into chapters later. We can't always know what order the chapters should be in until we have it written out on paper. I just like to write whatever rolls of my tongue and let the rest work itself out from there. I say to follow whichever path fits you best and to be flexible and to evolve with the project.

Following the path of least resistance and simplifying is also about pursuing the most realistic ways to become wealthy in order to manifest your fortune which we will go over in chapter thirteen ahead. Before we go over that, however, you can't pursue these wealth avenues without the right can-do attitude and finding your inspiration through the power of mantras ahead.

Eli Scott |

Wealth Principle 11

The power of mantras

Our greatest glory is not in never falling, but in rising every time we fall.
-Confucius

The beginning is the most important part of the work. -Plato

As I said at the end of wealth principle five, there are other ways that you can use the law of attraction in your thoughts, beliefs, and can-do attitude to bring fortune to you and one way you can do that is through the power of mantras. As preachy and cheesy as this principle will sound, using mantras that you can post on your walls will be one of the most powerful things you can do in attracting wealth to you. But how and why is this technique so powerful in making you wealthy? Although you cannot simply wish or pray for a vault of gold to magically appear for you, doing this one thing gives the most successful people the daily motivation, strength, encouragement, positivity, reminders, and inspiration to pursue their wealthy endeavors everyday. Additionally, mantras remind you of who you are, what you can do, what is possible for you, and helps you to stay focused everyday in order to "attract" what it is that you want to you. Even statisticians say that the chances of people taking action increases significantly when they see posters or flyers to encourage them to do the things that people want them to do, and your chances of becoming a millionaire increase one hundred fold when you see these mantras on your walls to empower and encourage you to seek your wealth for you.

Now do I think there is a chance that I wouldn't be where I'm at today without these mantras to help me? Yes, I absolutely think that I would have never found my own personal success in becoming wealthy if I did not use this technique to empower me. Of course I didn't use these law of attraction tricks forever, but only as long as it took to jump start my ambitions and to give me the mentality and willpower to keep working at it everyday. I only had to keep these mantras up for about two years before I no longer needed them to inspire me in which I became self empowered to keep working at my endeavor.

So what is a mantra? While various online dictionaries may define this as words or formulas that are repeated (in some cases to aid meditation), the sorts of mantras I am referring to are simply words of inspiration against any negativities or to just give you enthusiasm and motivation to work at your endeavors everyday. I personally took a marker to gift wrapping paper or poster paper that I bought at the dollar discount store, and wrote the things that would remind me what I was capable of doing and give me the most strength to continue pursuing further everyday. While you can look up various inspirational quotes of your own online that resonate with you the most, some of the mantras I posted on my bedroom walls were

"Feel the fear and do it <u>anyway</u>"

"There's no try, you <u>Do</u>"

"Everyday is the beginning"

"Fall flat on your face"

And

"Do what no one else will".

I found these mantras to be very powerful in which the most powerful one to me was "Fall flat on your face". Now what do I mean by that and why was that so inspirational for me? Fall flat on your face means going to the extreme in doing whatever it takes to make your wealth a reality for you regardless of the risks* you take and how stupid or embarrassed you may feel in doing so. It means to go all the way in and not half way in on whatever it is that you set out to do. It means to do whatever it takes period and you need to not be discouraged and keep doing and trying regardless of your fears, doubts, and other people's negativity toward you and no matter how many times you fail at your attempts to become successful.

I would also like to briefly discuss the mantra that says "everyday is the beginning", and what that means is that you have to be a self starter to ignite your fire every single day to get there. There is no one else that forces or motivates you to go to work at it everyday but yourself, and this is where you have to find the discipline to just do it through the lack of progress you see in it each day. This is one of the most difficult things that any self enterpriser can run into and this is where you have to go back to how badly you want it that will motivate you in doing so.

In addition to putting mantras on your walls, there are many other methods to this law of attraction trick. It has been said that some rich and famous people (who were not born into money) wrote a fake check to themselves for a million dollars or more before they became successful to incite their own law of attraction that they were going to be rich and successful one day. This technique is powerful in that it makes their wealth more real to them in which they then strive harder for that million dollars to come to them. Remember that you are what you eat and that you do based on what you think is real for you.

By the way, if you read my first book Think and Be Rich and The Portal to Financial Gold, you may have noticed that I use some of the same quotes in this book as I did in that one. I decided that this was fine as it coincides with this wealth principle. You may have also noticed that I underlined a word in two of my mantras above which can make powerful words stick out to you.

You can also find inspiration and motivation by idolizing other rich people. Remember how I mentioned that you must obsess over becoming rich in wealth principle one? Money and becoming rich must be what you think about and focus on at all times, and obsessing over other rich people's wealth can help keep you focused on building wealth. While there are many ways you can idolize those people, I did so by looking up famous people's net worth online a few times a week. Even if they are not close to being accurate numbers, most of these people are still multi- millionaires and seeing any amount of other people's wealth inspires me to strive for their wealth status.

You can also put sticky notes everywhere from your bathroom mirrors, fridge, or sun visor that can say anything from I can do it, I will do it, I am going to be rich, I am already a millionaire, I'm worth ten million dollars, people will like me, people will listen to me, people will buy from me, be willing to fail over and over, or whatever you want to post that inspires you against other people's or your own negativity and doubts toward you. I would be cautious about putting any mantras or sayings of any sort on your work space as I felt that one of my bosses successfully sought my termination when they saw that I was more focused on other things outside of work. People will find any reason to get you fired, especially when they are after your job or your salary in bonus money. I know from experience!

These were all powerful techniques that I personally used to arouse my own energy and motivation to work at my endeavors despite my own fears, negativities, doubts, and laziness to work at them every day and regardless of what my naysayers had to say. However, there was another powerful trick that I used in empowering myself to keep doing regardless of any naysayers or discouragement toward me. It is by doing this that will then allow you to pursue the real ways to get wealthy by building a stomach of steel and beating negativity out of you in the next wealth principle ahead.

*Although you cannot get anywhere without taking risks, I would never encourage anyone to take full blown risks and put their lives or their children's lives at risk. There is such thing as taking mitigated risks as we will discuss further in the last chapter.

Eli Scott |

Wealth Principle 12

Build a stomach of steel against negativity and doubt

He who has conquered doubt and fear has conquered failure. -James Lane Allen

To avoid criticism, do nothing, say nothing, and be nothing. -Elbert Hubbard

So as we went over in the earlier wealth principles, you will always have people who only want to tear and beat you down and that those who are the closest to you will be your biggest naysayers in your wealthy endeavors. And so how do we keep pursuing our wealth path through other people's negativity toward us. We find the strength to pursue through what our naysayers say by simply reflecting it. However, rich people once again take this to the extreme. What rich people do that poor people don't is that they are fully resistant and immune to their naysayers by simply ignoring them.

Rich people simply don't listen to most people because everyone and their next door neighbor is automatically going to be discouraging toward them. The majority of the population is raised and groomed to be nothing but negative, rejecting, and skeptical of everything. It's as if our forefathers intended that we learn negativity before positivity in our daily endeavors. When you think about it, one of the shortest and simplest words to say and one of the first that we learn at a very young age is the word "no". As a case in point, the word "no" is one of the very few words that my one year old niece knows how to say in which she says all day long now: "no no no no no!", but she doesn't even know how to say the word yes! Furthermore, most people are not rich as I mentioned in wealth principle three in which they will all have limiting beliefs in themselves and others.

It is with all of this then that you understand that negativity prevails in almost everyone and is going to be one of the most common things we encounter in which you don't listen to any of them. You need not think anything of it when they reject you or incite a lot of fear and doubt in you.

No matter who you are or what you do, you are going to have criticism with anything you do in which you might as well be doing something rather than nothing and learn to not let any of this negativity phase you in pursuing your wealth path regardless of who you are and how unlikely you think it is to become wealthy. The only thing that is going to stop you is your limiting beliefs in what you can do in which I say those who get rich don't believe in any of their naysayers and plow through to their dreams and desires. Disregard what they think or say to you no matter what it is and continue to pursue. This is the best thing you can do in order to prevail through your ambitions for you. However, if you can't ignore these people and what they say to you then you can also follow my next suggestion in building resistance to it.

While there are a few ways that you can build resistance to other people's negativity, the first thing that rich people do is to beat the negativity back out of them. Those who don't do this never become wealthy because they let other people's negative opinions and beliefs form their opinions and beliefs as to who we are and what we are capable of doing. Words are very powerful in convincing our minds as to what we can't achieve for ourselves. This is where you need to be more stubborn that you can do regardless of what people tell you and to not let their words eat at you. And the only way you can do that is to be above the negative and limiting words that swell in your head and beat them right back out of you.

This is one of the easiest things to do through what I call a rap battle between yourself and the thoughts in your head. Every time a negative thought, feeling, or doubt comes to the forefront of your head, you simply reject these negative thoughts and then lift yourself with encouragement to you. When you think things like I'm too stupid to do this or I will never be smart enough, no one will ever listen to me, I am not capable, it's too hard, it's too difficult, I can't do it, I won't do it, it's not real, it's not possible, I don't have the means, I will never be that, no one will like me, no one will accept me, I won't be rich or successful, I wont achieve my goals, or I'll never be, you repeatedly combat it with the exact opposite until you no longer have a single negative thought in your head. For example, you say to yourself things like I am smart enough, people will listen to me, people do like me, people will like what I have to offer, I can do that, I will be rich, I don't care what other people think of me, I will achieve that, I will find a way and I'll get there no matter what it takes, etc.

Battling your own negativity out of your head can be a very challenging experience as you have to be very firm and persistent with it, but it can also be very rewarding. By doing this one exercise alone, I found so much faith in lifting myself up with the empowered beliefs that I too was going to be something big someday and achieve the dreams of my desires. But it wasn't my own encouragement that gave me the idea to battle other people's scathing criticism toward me. I had read many inspiring books by that point which all had the same moral to the story: grow a backbone! By growing my own backbone, I was able to build full resistance and immunity to other people's negativity and limitations for me. They would throw it at me and it wouldn't even phase me. It also helps to remember that these are other people's negative thoughts and not your own in which you know they know nothing and aren't willing to do what you will to be rich and wealthy.

Those who learn how to beat negativity out of them also learn to reflect it by building a stomach of steel against it as your stomach can also heavily swell inside you in which it can then overpower you. Building a stomach of steel is again very easy to do in which you take all of that negativity, fear and doubt that builds up in your stomach and push it right back out of you by tightening your stomach muscles and "forcing" those feelings out of you. I can't really tell you how to do it you just do. You then firmly empower yourself in your get rich beliefs and encouragement for you. While doing these two things are easy to do, you only need to do them a few times to build your ultimate empowerment for you, however, you should do them as many times as you need to until the negative thoughts from yourself and others are no longer a thought that comes to you.

Now again do I think I would be wealthy today if I didn't take it upon myself to stubbornly ignore and deflect other people's limits for me? Absolutely not, because I knew that I would have let these things paralyze me. But I told myself that if I ever wanted to be rich and wealthy, I had to conquer these fears and doubts and blast through my own disbeliefs as well as other people's criticism and discouragement in becoming wealthy. With that, I was able to work towards my goals everyday with full force that I was absolutely going to be rich someday.

While these techniques are meant to empower you through your personal obstacles or challenges, they are not meant to get around barriers in enterprising you. Knowing the difference between the two can help you to determine what endeavors to pursue in which we now dive into the most realistic ways to become wealthy in the next wealth principle ahead.

Eli Scott |

Wealth Principle 13

Find the realistic ways to become wealthy

Success is dependent on effort. -Sophocles

Although we just went over building resistance to discouragement from the majority of people around you in the last wealth principle, I am going to contradict myself for only a moment when I say that there are times when your friends and family can be right in regards to your limitations in pursuing wealth systems. While you have to remain stubborn in your can-do attitude to become wealthy, you can still fail when you are doing things that are either unrealistic or have too many barriers to their success. Even business management courses in marketing, product development, and innovation go over entry barriers as well as the many things that can destruct or disrupt even existing multibillion dollar corporations which is why this is so important in briefing over here.

The point of this is not to discourage you from working around your obstacles or challenges which you can conquer, but to learn your limits and barriers in enterprising you. By doing so, you can determine when you need to stop pursuing certain things that won't get you there so that you can pursue the things that can bring millions to you. The best way to achieve this is to of course pursue the most realistic ways to get wealthy which we will get to in a minute, and to thoroughly research anything that you set out to do.

If you don't think that researching and knowing your barriers are important in determining your money making opportunities to you, then here is a short story about my friend John who had to disrupt the business of real estate investors who were renting out homes short term in his neighborhood which resulted in increased theft and vandalism within the neighborhood. The city these homes resided in had already banned short term rentals to any dwellings where it was not the owner's primary residence due to increased crime from these types of rentals. All John had to do was report this illegal activity to the city to stop this illegal activity of investors renting out homes short term. John and his neighbors, however, chose to ban these types of rentals through their HOA and successfully stopped the crime in their area. In this case, HOA bylaws are allowed to be retroactively implemented after the HOA and its original rules had been established anytime it's meant to combat crime or the threat to the condition and value to the homes it's meant to protect.

So when you are looking for ways to become wealthy, don't think that you can just start any business, franchise, real estate endeavor, start-up, or any money making opportunity without researching everything that is involved in running a smooth money making machine, because it's not as easy as buying real estate that you think you can just rent out short term when some cities and HOA's have already or can illegalize/ban them. This is also why I highly recommend not trying to launch new ideas or any business without taking courses in business administration and management. You don't have to get a full degree from a college, but even completing a few free or cheap certificate programs online in these subjects can be very powerful for you.

Many of the other business barriers and challenges that they teach in business courses have been developed into models, graphs, and formulas that include PEST (political, economic, social, technological) issues, SWOT analysis, porter's five forces, and the BCG growth share matrix amongst others. Additionally, many types of businesses in franchising, real estate, or e-commerce to name a few can carry personal barriers and limits in that they all require your constant hustle around the clock and relying on hundreds of people who all carry the same mindset as you in making them functional. You can also get way over your head in that they can be too expensive, too complicated, and too time consuming for you. At the end of the day, none of these things are feasible for most people.

Finally, no one gets rich from simply investing their money. The only people who get rich off of investments are those who are already wealthy and have a lot of money to put into investments in which they can gain significant ownership in that stock and in which they can in many cases protect their investments from dilution. Most people, however, have a very small ownership stake in their public investments and are usually subject to massive dilution as the company sells more stocks to people. Additionally, most investments can take seven to ten years to double depending on expenses, fees, and return rate on the fund. So don't think you can just simply put five hundred to one thousand dollars into any investment even if it's real estate and think that you will ever become rich and wealthy.

So this now brings us to the most realistic ways to get wealthy through personal finance. In my book Think and Be Rich and the Portal to Financial Gold, I discuss what I call the Bermuda Triangle which explains how masses of money gets drained from your wallet by invisible forces that lie right underneath you in every transaction you make or sign into that can completely destroy you. It is by learning these important money management and preservation principles that you can learn how to protect hundreds of thousands of dollars which is critical for leveraging your income for you. Even the largest corporations and richest investors and entrepreneurs follow the principle to conserve their personal and business cash in every way possible through personal financial management and by developing lean start-ups with minimum viable products.

To leverage your income means to multiply your earnings either through large sales or by building multiple active and passive residual monthly income streams from the jobs, side hustles, and investments that provide that. Active income is working many hours to get a small one time paycheck to come to you and you have to keep working everyday to continue getting paid. Passive Income is working hard for only a couple of years until you can build automatic income in leveraging your money for you. An example of active income is working at a nine to five job and an example of passive income is that in rental income or royalties. Although passive income may seem like it's easier than active income, they are both necessary in securing your financial future by building residual income for you. Passive income can also be just as difficult as you have to work hard to build passive systems for you.

You can leverage your income by buying and selling real estate (although there's no guaranteed winning strategy), and putting hundreds of thousands of dollars into leveraged investments with high earning potential. These types of investments are most of the time found through private holdings that are sold prior to initial public offering (IPO), however, you often times must meet the accredited investor requirements to go into most of these types of investments**. For those who don't know what IPO is, that is when a company goes public to sell it's shares to the general mass public. You want to get into private high net worth investments before they go public as shares can dilute massively once they sell to the public. These types of investments are considered very risky, however, which is why you need to be sure to work with properly licensed brokers and lawyers who can best advise you with these as well as the best investment rounds to go into. D and E rounds are generally less risky than pre-seed and A-C rounds.

Another way to leverage your income is to invest in rental units that can bring monthly residuals back to you. However, this is most of the time not considered passive income, meaning it's not quick or easy, because you can't just put your money into a real estate investment managed by other people and expect that you will receive reward without a lot of risk. While there is no guaranteed winning strategy with this, those who do this might either want to manage their own real estate units or be actively involved in managing these with a team of people in which you are sure to have enough ownership that you will have control over the strategies employed. This means that the people who succeed with these the most hustle to bring in active income.

Income and savings are again the most important things you need in order to leverage your money through these various means, but savings is about more than not spending on basic things. Those who win the most are those who pay attention to the experts on when to not buy appliances or cars, what cars you shouldn't buy as they will bankrupt you on repairs, when to not buy car warranties, what not to buy at bulk membership discount clubs, and the jobs that will be gone in the next ten years. Rich people don't buy expensive clothes, cars, jewelry, furniture, or appliances until they are rich and wealthy. They also pay attention to the prestigious organizations such as Blackrock in regards to the housing market and as preachy as this sounds, they are smart about being with the significant others who don't drain all their money.

Other realistic ways to become wealthy involve going to school and getting jobs at the highest paying career fields in medicine, engineering, and technology. They work in teams at high earning positions. Those who work the hardest in the jobs or high net worth enterprises that pay the most (distinguished engineers, medical doctors, lawyers, Silicon Valley technologists, and national correspondents) are the ones who get rewarded the most. Additionally, it has been noted by many experts that side hustles are significant in increasing your overall wealth to you.

On a final note, those who lose the most are those who put their money into the wrong financial policies.

Financial wealth consultants of many sorts prey on desperate people to sell various financial policies that are not always in the best interest of people. It's up to you to determine if life insurance policies and annuities are really in your best interests or if they are just meant to take a lot of your hard earned money. These types of policies can in some cases be no different than you giving your savings to someone else to manage in which they decide how much of your money they keep and what to pay back to you and most of the time they simply keep the majority of it while giving a small portion of your money back to you. Now I'm not saying anything here about these products that I'm not allowed to. The disadvantages of these various types of products to include lots of fees with very low returns is even taught in securities licensing courses. In the end, there is no such thing as a magic money and savings vehicle except the one where you manage it yourself and if you can't save or manage your money well, talk to your banker about ways to help you without buying into other predatory policies that are only meant to victimize you. Be careful about putting your money into money market CD's as they can keep you from investing in other opportunities when they are locked for ninety days or more.

It is also best to talk to several independent financial brokers who all work out of their own firms to help analyze the best policies for you. Pay attention to how they receive commissions from the policies they sell to you. If they work with a big national chain of brokers then they may be biased in pushing predatory products onto you as they have to make more money for their up line. Find the broker who works alone and not in these networks who only want to take a lot of your hard earned money from you. You will know if they work for a network if they work to recruit advisors and brokers underneath them.

Those who learn not to give their money to the wrong financial policies out of desperation also don't pursue the wrong things for the wrong reasons in order to become wealthy which we now embark on in the next wealth principle titled you cannot compete for the wrong jobs ahead.

* What is a private wealth manager?

A private wealth manager is someone who has the proper financial licenses to help make you money by brokering with institutions and investments that carry low fees and expenses such as index funds whereas other types of brokers may work with investments that research has shown can deflate a significant amount of your investments over a lifetime from excessive and expensive fees. Private wealth managers also usually tend to work with clients who are already wealthy or work to put clients in accredited private high end investments that you must qualify for as mandated through the Securities Exchange Commission. You can find financial calculators that can help you project the total costs of your investments over a lifetime.

** One consideration for the accreditation requirements is that you can hold a series 65 license and be in good standing with a professional finance position. You don't have to be employed with a firm to test for your series 65 exam and you can find organizations and groups who will let you independently advise with them in order to qualify as an accredited investor.

Eli Scott |

Wealth Principle 14

_____

You cannot compete for the wrong jobs

Think for yourself or others will think for you without thinking of you. -Henry David Thoreau

This principle is once again not for the average person and is one of the most powerful wealth principles which is that you cannot compete for the wrong jobs, however, rich people once again go to the extreme with this. Rich people don't strive to get hired or promoted at just any job for the sake of the job and instead focus on only things that will make them rich. This means they are not competitive with other people to try to up them in the careers that they strive for. As I said previously, rich people don't care about matching their image with other people. They also don't strive to be "important" by having fancy job titles and don't compare themselves with anyone who is getting those "glamorous" careers and jobs that they are not. The people who do strive for those careers are meant to focus on those careers to make a living. Furthermore, they are not willing to do what you are in order to become massively wealthy and that means staying narrowly focused on your goals and endeavors that will make you wealthy and taking the huge risks that you need to in order to get there.

So now that we have this concept down, I will describe the extreme measures I took to stay focused on my wealthy endeavors. For me this meant not enhancing my skill sets anywhere and working at the bottom of the chain at all of my hourly jobs. By focusing on enhancing my career, I would have spent all of my free time and mental energy working up at a job to increase my yearly salary by one to ten thousand dollars a year -OR- I could do what I did instead and spend all of my free time and mental energy on the avenues that would explode my wealth. In the process, I had to not care about what everyone else around me was doing in their work promotions and new job titles and I had to remind myself that I was going to be rich someday and that they were most likely ninety nine percent of a chance not ever going to be!

Going to the extreme for me also meant not going back to school for anything that I did not care about, refusing to go into management, refusing to do continuing education programs, and refusing to earn any professional licenses that would only distract me. Now I'm not saying you shouldn't climb the ladder at jobs that can pay you a lot of money but quite the contrary. There are many people who become wealthy by climbing the ladder at their jobs be it medical doctors, founders and CEO's, distinguished engineers, executive producers and directors, technology professionals and managers, and any other high paying jobs you can think of that has made other people wealthy. I knew that climbing the ladder somewhere was not my personal wealth avenue, however, and therefore intentionally focused on the avenues that I felt were my wealth path.

Those who get rich also don't get resentful of the job positions they don't get and stay focused on their goal. When my entrepreneurial endeavors came to a lull in my mid thirties, I decided to go back to school for a degree in digital marketing and content strategy in which I then applied for a job that would pay me forty thousand dollars a year. Unfortunately, I had not ever heard back from that employer after my first interview in which I became disappointed, discouraged, and jealous over whoever did get it. I was also angry and embarrassed that I didn't land the position. However, I immediately rebounded from these thoughts and feelings when it was around that same time that I started to see my endeavors take off for me in which I had realized that this path was only going to distract me. I solidified my thoughts in telling myself that this is not what my goals were in becoming wealthy and am now in the process of doing what it is that will. Additionally, I was already making more money at my part time pizza delivery job than that job offered me!* I am also sure that employer never called me back because they could see that I was not that serious about that job when I wasn't making a serious effort in pursuing it.

This is the same mindset you need to have when you are going for the wrong things for the wrong reasons. Do not look for the degrees, jobs, or job titles that won't serve you and go for the money making opportunities that will. Don't be hurt when employers refuse to hire you because you are focusing on the things that will get you wealthy instead. Furthermore, be happy for the people around you who do get those promotions that you didn't or never will, because someday you will have what they never will!

Now this principle is not saying to not be desperate for a job. Unless you were born into money, everyone has to make a living and there's nothing wrong with being desperate for something that will give you a paycheck to live and survive. What this principle is saying is to not heavily concentrate on the jobs that will take up a lot of your time and energy and essentially warp your mind and distract you from pursuing the things that will make you wealthy. Additionally, you should only limit your career opportunities if you know for sure you can become wealthy through other avenues as it can be highly risky.

Those who get wealthy also don't get jealous or resentful of other successful people who beat them to their ideas. Those who become rich keep going with building their wealth for them even when they lose out on opportunities. Rich people cannot be jealous of anything and get past the coulda woulda shoulda of everything and they instead find ways to pivot off of other ideas to advance them or simply make them more appealing to people. Additionally, there already has to be a proven market and other people doing the same thing as you in order to build trust and traction with consumers. So you need to be happy and encouraged when there's other people doing the same thing as you. Use saturated and crowded markets in your favor to become wealthy.

Rich people also know that they can't be the one to develop inventions and instead look for the "right" start-ups to invest in. My biggest regret is not that I didn't invent Tik Tok, even though I thought of it well before it was created, but that I didn't research to see if other people were doing it and invest into it early stage before stocks were open to the public. However, in hindsight, I don't really know that this would have been a great investment either. Remember that all investments come with risk and I would have had to pull out of the investment at the perfect timing in order to cash in on it.

Those who are willing to go to the extreme to pursue wealth systems must have extreme patience and faith in their endeavors which we now discuss in the next wealth principle ahead.

*Can you really make that much money as a pizza delivery driver?

The short answer to this is both yes and no. How much money you can make being a pizza delivery driver can vary based on many factors and not all positions are equal. How much money you can make doing that depends on the specific employer and location you work for. You can potentially make more money delivering pizza than you can working at a desk job if you find an employer who guarantees you a position of a minimum of thirty hours a week and who won't reduce your hours for new hires. You also need to look for the employers who pay you decent mileage as well as in-store wages (as opposed to tipped wages only). I had better luck in a ritzy neighborhood with tip payouts than I did in a less ritzy one. You also need to work for the employer who will pay you a five dollar credit or the original tip payout on top of mileage when you have to retake mistakes made by other employees or other food delivery drivers that the employer uses. Another thing to keep in mind is that delivery driving is listed as one of the top ten most dangerous jobs in America due to accidents, robberies, and assaults, so use extreme caution when deciding to take on a job of this nature as well as the cities and neighborhoods you choose to work in. Also, if you do choose to work in this type of job, be prepared to work for some of the most unprofessional in-store and upper level managers who do not manage their stores well or address problems in appropriate ways which can lead to rising tensions and fights amongst managers and co-workers.

Eli Scott |

Wealth Principle 15

You must have patience and faith

The only time you run out of chances is when you stop taking them.
-Alexander Pope
Don't judge each day by the harvest you reap but by the seeds that you plant.
-Robert Louis Stevenson
It does not matter how slowly you go as long as you do not stop. -Confucius

One of the hardest things that self made millionaires must do is to confidently pursue their get rich endeavors when they are discouraged by their current circumstances they are living in. For example, it is hard for most people to believe that they will ever become rich when they don't see the money coming in right away and don't have a wealthy lifestyle. Furthermore, we all have friends and family discouraging us even more when they tell us that if we haven't done it by now we're never going to which enforces our beliefs that becoming rich will never happen. So those who will win at this get rich game are the ones who hold extreme patience to pursue through their unfortunate circumstances which is the number one thing that will determine your wealth for you. Through this process, you have to trust what you are doing and have to remain persistent in your attitude and beliefs in amassing your wealth to you because it takes a lot of dedication and unwavering faith that you will achieve your success for you. When I speak of faith, I don't mean in that of religion or a belief in God, but that in which you put full belief in yourself and what you do to enterprise you.

While you can find your own ways to find your patience and faith in in all, I did so by simply repeating the word "patience" a few times a week and it was as if someone from above was talking to me from the skies and ensuring me that I would be rich someday. I held my own long lasting faith in all of my endeavors that I would get there no matter how long it took and no matter how difficult it was in perspiring through it all. I also knew that I was meant to be here in this world to do something big, I just didn't know what and I trusted self guidance on whatever it was that I needed to do to get there.

Now I'm not saying that I did this without any of the severe uncertainty that came with it. I had a lot of fear and anxiety as my gut wrenched everyday through the pain and despair of it all, but I wouldn't have gotten there without the extreme faith and patience in doing it. Day after day, I had to keep the extreme patience and trust the process in which I would then one day realize my prosperity in it all, and this is what you must do every single day no matter how difficult and tedious it is and no matter how long it takes in building your empire. Building your wealth is like gathering tinder for a campfire. It's not something that you receive a paycheck for in the beginning, but as planting your seeds until one day you ignite a ginormous bonfire in which your fortune explodes in massive royalties or profits that come to you later. Even the most famous billionaires have to do this as many of them are actually broke and in debt as their billions of dollars are wrapped up in unrealized shares that they can't cash out on through the entirety of building and running their billion dollar companies.

So you too must have the same mindset with your ventures that you are not going to reap profit immediately, but that you are everyday planting the seeds that you need to that will one day magically bring royalties and fortune to you, even if it takes ten to twenty years in doing so. Those who get rich also say to themselves I'm a millionaire now but I just won't see it for another two to five or even forty years from now! You must remain patient and keep going and taking the next step in your endeavors through the madness of it all. When you are failing, go one step further. When you are confused, go one step further. When you are in despair, exhausted, in fear and doubt, and have no idea where you are going, go one step further. Regardless of how many times you fail, everything will eventually come together. I failed thousands of times and yet kept going at finding the one thing that would some day make me wealthy. It is only by doing and challenging that you can accomplish your wealth for you and then to have the complete faith through the lack of what you have and the negativity around you that you must persevere through to see your own success for you. The key is to keep working at it every day no matter how long it takes to gather your tinder and plant your seeds until you build your wealth empire.

This now brings me to a short story I share with you about the tale of the Cheetah and the Cricket. These are two characters who were featured in my book Think and Be Rich and the Portal to Financial Gold. To give a quick background of these two characters, the Cheetah is the one who runs as fast as she can toward her pot of gold while avoiding distractions or the bait of bright shiny objects that are only meant to drain her money from her, and the Cricket is the one who hops from corner to corner to collect his gold. Of particular significance here is where they talk about finding their own faith to persevere through. It is with this that I start with the Cheetah in which I let her tell her story:

"I was once the girl like you looking for my golden treasure when I lost all faith in my endeavor.

When you look up into the starry night skies, you have no idea how you will ever fly. You lose all hope in what you do and have no idea if you will pull through. It was through this adversity that I laid in my bed and looked up at the night sky in which a big air balloon came over me and said 'When you lose faith in your journey and don't know what to do, hold onto me and I will carry you through.' As you set out on your journey, you will learn how to build your blades of steel which will propel this ship through. Although I didn't know if I would ever find my gold, I let everlasting faith carry me fourfold. When you lack faith in your endeavor, you build four steel blades that last forever. And by building your own system that flies, you will soar through the never ending skies."

The big air balloon in this case represents all of your knowledge, skills, and experience that will carry you through in manifesting wealth for you. But there are many different ways that one can find faith in which the Cricket tells a different story:

"While the Cheetah found her faith in a big air balloon, I found my faith by just persevering through. It doesn't matter what tricks we impart to you, it is only your heart that will carry you through. It is when you master these tricks that we scry onto you that you will build your own set of propellers and simply glide through. Once you've found your fierce passion and reason for doing whatever you set out to do, nothing will stop you from doing everything it takes to persevere through. Those who win at this get rich game simply just do".

If you too want to become wealthy, then you just have to do in which you find your way to find faith to persevere through. It is only the systems in that which you either find severe passion in or that you find a severe reason to do, that the enterprise will move you.

However, no matter how much you seek these things, you may never succeed until you have the number one thing you need to become wealthy in the next wealth principle ahead.

Eli Scott |

Wealth Principle 16

_____

The number one thing you need to become wealthy

Educating the mind without educating the heart is no education at all. -Aristotle

What do you think is the number one thing that can bring your ultimate wealth to you?

While the answer to this is debatable, I would say that your overall health will be the number one thing you must have in arousing the energy and focus needed in manifesting your ultimate wealth to you. So what do I mean by overall health? While health is a diverse subject matter that can be achieved through several means, I am going to start off with your physical health. Now don't worry as I'm not telling you to become a health freak by any means as I certainly am not. I do not exercise as much as I should and I still eat burgers and fries like everyone else, but why would my physical health be so important in attracting my fortune to me? While sparing you the intimate details, I have had a few near death experiences in my lifetime, some which were a result of poor physical health. It is for this reason that I like to stay healthy in order to continue doing this thing called life. It is your physical health that you can't function without and what allows you to aspire to your fullest potential. With all of that being said however, I cannot tell anyone how to become physically healthy or maintain physical health as I am not qualified to do so. You can talk with your doctor as well as other qualified physicians about how to be physically healthy and you should always consult a doctor before starting any nutrition or exercise program.

Maintaining my physical health also meant cutting alcohol out of my life completely as I couldn't function when I was physically intoxicated. Now I know that there are lots of social and occasional drinkers out there who are saying yeah right I'm not giving up my alcohol, and that's fine. I have been there and done that and I know how you feel. I also know it's not as easy as just telling you to quit drinking. The decision or ability to cut alcohol out of your life can be a very complicated matter and what motivates a person to quit drinking is going to be different for everyone. However, those who are dead serious about becoming wealthy will naturally find themselves cutting alcohol out of there lives so that they can stay focused on their endeavors. I could not limit or control my drinking and therefore chose to give up alcohol completely.

Now going over the necessity of your physical health is only scratching the surface of your overall health to you. Our overall health is also about balancing all areas of your life together in that of home and family as well as our mental, emotional, and spiritual health. It is also about being happy with ourselves and having all of our needs met and achieving that which we desire. Your overall health is also about finding complete wholeness within yourself. In much shorter terms, it just means to find yourself and your life. It means to find your home and belonging in life. It means to feed the inner you to do what it is that you like. It means to be involved with family and community, and it means to just have the life that you desire. It also means to get rid of toxic people and things that are not serving you as we went over in wealth principle eight. Only be with the person who is going to uplift and support you in your ambitions everyday.

In the process of doing the things that will bring your overall health to you, you do not want to get confused with the things that won't. Arousing your overall health is not about giving into your bad habits or unhealthy vices. A lot of these things just drain your bank account and keep you from focusing on your goals, especially in the case of substances, leaving you anxious and unfulfilled in which you never find your path for you. Rather, you can arouse your overall health in mind, body, and soul by doing a bunch of healthy activities in hobbies, community, and recreation that nourish ourselves on all levels. You can also arouse your overall health through doing the things that nourish you and being true to yourself first. Being true to yourself allows you to release any unnecessary obligations in your life in which you don't have to please or impress other people and you can do what you want, not what others want for you. Releasing these obligations then allows doors to open for you because you will have more time and room to work on the things that will enterprise you.

You do this by not listening to others and listening to yourself on what you want in life that will give you the direction you need to enterprise you. It is within listening to and following your true heart that will arouse your passion and allow you to pursue what you do.

As silly as all of these things sound, ask yourself how happy you are and if you have the life you desire? We can find ourselves doing the wrong things for the wrong reasons living to please or impress others. So if you want to become wealthy, consider reflecting on your true self and bringing all areas of your life into balance. Find your own motivation to give up all of your own vices that can stall you in pursuing your wealth be it booze, recreational drugs, TV, and video games. It all comes back to how badly you want it as we went over in wealth principle six, and finding that one thing that will make you wealthy. Additionally, as I mention in wealth principle number four, you don't have to cut any of these vices out of your life forever but long enough to do what it takes to get to your golden treasure. You also don't want to quit anything cold turkey or just swiftly eliminate them from your life because we can experience shock or withdrawals by doing so. You want to instead start by adding things into your life that will be of greatness to you and when you do, you may find prosperity to come to you.

Now to put a twist onto all of this, people who get rich are those who don't let anything, be it excuses or their overall health stop them. It is my opinion that everything has a reciprocal effect on one another and this is no exception. Sometimes we have to fight through the battle first regardless of any of these things to achieve our end game. Furthermore, we cannot find our overall health, our desired lifestyle and belonging until we have achieved that which will bring the life that we desire. So you may find yourself working until you're sick as a dog and also taking breaks to find your heart in it all. This would explain why it may seem like I am contradicting myself from the beginning of this book which is that you have to ignore everyone and everything in your life in order work around the clock to enterprise you, and that you must be extreme in not finding balance in your life in order to become wealthy. Fighting through the battle will be the ultimate key to manifesting your fortune which now brings us to the number one reason you will fail in the next wealth principle ahead.

Eli Scott |

Wealth Principle 17

The number one reason you will fail

Never leave that till tomorrow which you can do today. - Benjamin Franklin
Energy and persistence conquer all things. -Benjamin Franklin

So now that we have gone over the number one thing that will bring wealth to you, what is the number one thing that will make you fail in your wealthy endeavors? After everything you have done to adopt the extreme lifestyle, behaviors, habits, and no-non sense attitude to do and have found that one thing that can make you wealthy, you may still find that you have no energy or motivation in doing it. There is only one more thing you need to get past in order to aspire and that is your procrastination or plain laziness in doing it. These two things will be the number one reason you will fail at anything and that will kill your chance of ever succeeding at your endeavors.

Now I will admit that I am no exception in having to deal with this in my enterprises. I am a huge offender of procrastination and laziness. No matter how much I wanted to launch any of my wealth making businesses, I found myself sitting on my couch for hours not working on any of them. Becoming a self made millionaire is one of the most difficult things in finding the motivation and willpower to do (after having kids, I hear some of you saying), as it comprises a lot of dedication to do, and yet I kept going and I kept working through the grueling intensity everyday. So how did I find the motivation past my laziness to work at my goals everyday? When you have done everything it takes to get the right mindset and seek the things that will make you wealthy, the only other thing you can do is to just force it. You have to be a warrior and you just have to do it. There is no nicer way to put it.

Why do I use the word warrior? No matter how badly we may want it, doing what it takes to become wealthy is not easy. The most successful people did not succeed by not working extremely hard for it and are the ones that persevere everyday in arousing their fortune. It's not easy working your butt off and it's not easy to work through the many painful challenges and obstacles you will have along the way. It is painful to do, it is painful to work through, and it is painful not knowing where any of it is going to get you. There are days that you will lose hope and faith in everything you do and you will have to sacrifice your life in the process. So no matter what reason you find to do, there is nothing more that will move you other than becoming a warrior to war through it with the discipline and perseverance of a ninja to do what it takes everyday to become wealthy.

Now I know this is easier said than done and so I will give a couple of my golden keys that I used to highly motivate me to just do through one simple step in simply opening my laptop everyday. I know this sounds really stupid, but this one little step forced me to look at my work items for five to ten minutes which then powerfully drew me in to work at them everyday. How is this silly and simple technique so powerful in motivating someone to do? It is all through the power of psychology. By staring at my laptop, I was able to keep my focus on what I was doing and why, and what the results would be if I did it. Additionally, when we find ourselves staring at things in front of us for ten minutes, our minds are programmed to challenge problems and to make progress. We are also naturally inclined to achieve and to make something of ourselves in which we naturally find ourselves doing what it is we set out to do.

In addition to this psychological trick, there is another powerful trick you can use with this technique to enhance your motivation in doing and that is through what I call using a super time clock. When I need to be motivated to start tapping away at my laptop to write, I set a twenty minute timer on my cell phone that psychologically moves me to power through an endeavor for that twenty minutes. Once the timer has run out, I then reset the timer for another twenty minutes and repeat every time it runs out as I continue to work for many hours on end. I think the reason this technique is so powerful is that it makes me feel less overwhelmed to work for only twenty minutes as opposed to three hours and once I get on a roll with twenty minutes I find myself to keep working well past that. This technique also works in that we are once again naturally challenged to race against the clock to champion our goals.

Along with putting off projects and goals, procrastination also involves everything that you can do to feel busy while not moving forward to act on the biggest action items that will enterprise you. This is among the top ten reasons start-ups can fail and can include doing things for the wrong reasons (procrastinating), reading rather than doing (procrastinating), and buying into more get rich systems while not taking action on them, in other words, procrastinating! Things that can be even more self sabotaging are when you procrastinate by trying to "know" everything and be perfect before you even build a business or market it and letting yourself get distracted by normal everyday things. Rather than wasting your time on such things, you need to be sure you are tackling the biggest items that will propel you to success every single day.

So how do you get past your own laziness to do? You just do and you power through like a warrior through all the pain and hard work it takes to enterprise you. And how do you not procrastinate? By ignoring all of the little things that only distract you and take massive action to do. Although taking care of important matters cannot be ignored, rich people don't let anything distract them from their wealthy endeavors and they don't try to know everything or be perfect. Poor people "need" to do everything other than their get rich systems and let themselves laze on the couch for hours. Rich people aggressively pursue their dreams at lightning-fast speed in which they don't even know what a couch is. So the next time you "need" to do something whether it's going through that junk drawer or doing routine chores or whatever it is that distracts you, you need to understand that you are doing nothing more than procrastinating from pursuing your wealthy endeavors.

We now only have a couple of wealth principles left that lead us to the number one secret to wealth in which we first go over the power of education and that you can become wealthy from any college and degree ahead.

Eli Scott |

Wealth Principle 18

You can become wealthy from any college and degree

An investment in knowledge pays the best interest. –Benjamin Franklin

While this chapter may seem a little boring, it is yet packed with powerful information in bringing wealth to you through an education. Those who go to college significantly increase their chances of becoming wealthy. However, you don't have to go to school to be a lawyer or doctor and you can become rich from any college or degree and with any grades you received in school. How can that be? Those who go to any college for any degree are the ones who take control and aspire at things that will make them wealthy and are the ones who make no excuses. A lot of poor people claim that they are poor because they grew up in poverty and didn't receive a good education. Did I grow up rich or receive a good education in school? Heck no. As a matter of fact, the education I received growing up was so terrible that I had no support from my parents or my teachers, and my grades severely suffered as a result. I also failed in all of the STEM subjects (science, technology, engineering, and math) that create the most amount of jobs and the jobs with the highest paying wages. However, I didn't let my lack of understanding of these subjects give me an excuse to not go to college anyways, even if I couldn't aspire at any of these high paying fields and even if I couldn't go to a prestigious college. So if you want to claim that you are poor because you didn't get a good education, don't have a good degree, or didn't go to a prestigious school, then you are letting excuses rule you while not taking the steering wheel to creating your own fortune.

While you don't have to get a full bachelor's degree in order to become wealthy, I fully believe that my bachelor's degree in political science highly contributed to my success by giving me the framework, discipline, knowledge and skills that I needed to succeed in the way that I did with my wealth enterprises. These are all of the valuable things that pay the most and helps to obtain your biggest asset as we discussed in wealth principle number five.

Not everyone just gets rich by being a "C" or "F" student in school and by going into real estate. While some money gurus claim that school doesn't teach money, those who succeed the most gain an education that can lead you to high wages that make some people wealthy and then learn how to leverage and diversify their money. So at the end of the day those who win at this game are those who build knowledge, skills, and experience and then work for the corporations that pay them in grand gold while also investing into real estate or other partnerships and alternative investments along the way.

It also doesn't matter where you go to school and what for. What matters is what you do and how well you do it. I know someone who I will call Jenna who makes over three hundred thousand dollars a year with a bachelor's degree in business and marketing from a state college. How is it that she makes this kind of money when most people with this same bachelors degree in business may never make more than sixty thousand dollars a year? The difference is that most people have very limited beliefs and knowledge in what they can do and go for normal minimum wage desk jobs after college in which they slowly work up the ranks at jobs that never spit back a lot of money. Jenna on the other hand went straight into an executive internship in her fourth year of college at a big retail giant. So the people who win at this get rich game don't at all get caught up in the nonsense of having to go to a prestigious college and make no excuses to winning their money. When you think about it, anyone can also go broke and poor after getting the most prestigious degrees from the most prestigious colleges. What matters is what you do with your college education and to not make any excuses.

To solidify this point, there are many employers who put no weight on prestigious schools at all in which they would prefer to hire people who went to low tier no name schools over those who went to elite colleges. Many recruiters claim that elite school graduates are the laziest workers because they let all of their ego get to their head in which they think they know everything and therefore don't need to do any work whereas those who graduated from no name schools are the hardest workers.

I have also come across many founders of successful tech companies and other six and seven figure earners throughout my lifetime who all received their college degrees from nationally accredited* or low tier technical colleges and trade schools that some people claim to be nothing more than diploma mills.

Additionally, my masters degree is from a foreign school that many United States citizens would criticize as poor quality as opposed to US schools, but why would I listen to these people who just want to encourage attending schools that charge hundreds of thousands of dollars from me? And it makes no sense to me how these self acclaimed online opinion forums (meaning no one qualifies their opinions but themselves) want to disqualify accredited foreign schools who use Harvard university content, but yet praise the non accredited degree of a school founded by one person who also disqualifies prestigious US schools. Are you confused? So am I. At the end of the day, these bashing games are no more than political mud slinging.

I also don't let not having a full bachelors degree in English or writing be the reason I can't be successful. As a case in point, one of the most powerful and beneficial courses I have taken for my career and wealth building was a specialization in writing and editing called Good with Words taught by Patrick Barry at the University of Michigan and provided by Coursera.org online. This course meant the difference of how to write my books in a way that would sell to people. This brings me to my next point that those who decide for absolute sure they are not going to pursue a bachelor's or other trade school degree should at least embark on free or cheap certificates and courses that you can get online from many different schools that can still give you the knowledge and discipline that you need to aspire. Taking courses from many schools can also provide a well rounded education with so much more information than what one school has to offer by itself. On a final note, many of the highest paid professionals in the world don't have any college degrees but take certificate programs online that can land them high paying jobs, usually in technology.

Now other get rich gurus teach you that getting rich is not about going to school in order to become rich and wealthy. You are taking a much bigger risk by not getting an education because you have nothing else to fall back on when all else fails. This get rich game is not about taking hard risk but rather mitigated risks to ensure a secure future for you. While many real estate tycoons want to preach that it's not about a secure paycheck, they are hypocrites in that they don't fully rely on their real estate portfolios. Most of them pad their wealth by either keeping their full time jobs or venturing out into other things such as education books and systems and or developing real estate software that they can sell to people.

A couple more things to think about is that some of the wealthiest people such as national news correspondents have bachelor's degrees in journalism, political science, business, or law and most giant tech founders have either bachelor's degrees or an equivalent education in engineering or physics. Finally, those who succeed the most learn how to influence and win people's hearts through their logic and compassion in what they say to people. Some of the wealthiest people in the world are those who learn how to write and speak to people in a way that sells. In other words, an education is powerful!

Now there is another characteristic that a lot of wealthy people carry. Those who are willing to be extremely silly can also significantly increase their wealth as we go over in the next wealth principle ahead.

*A quick word on accreditation

So does accreditation really matter when it comes to choosing your degrees and schools? The very quick answer to this is, it depends on the profession that you choose. Nowadays, a lot of professional degrees or certificates don't need to be from accredited schools anymore and as a case in point, most certificate programs that universities roll out now are not accredited at all. The universities themselves are accredited, but their certificate programs are not. So whether you need to attend an accredited school or have an accredited degree really depends on what you are going to school for and what you are going to do with your degree. Also know that hospitals do hire medical staff who have nationally accredited and not regionally accredited degrees. A lot of technology degrees and certificates are also not accredited and don't necessarily need to be.

Eli Scott |

Wealth Principle 19

You must be willing to be extremely silly

While this wealth principle is going to be again very short, it will be one of the most significant in becoming wealthy and that is, you must be willing to be silly. But some of the wealthiest people once again take this to the extreme. What rich people are willing to do that poor people are not is that of going way outside the norm in their actions and endeavors in bringing in millions or even billions of dollars to them. They will also do so at the cost of embarrassment which they once again don't let stop them. So now what do I mean by being extremely silly? There are many ways that one can be silly in their millionaire vocations to them but to make things simple, let's start with the most obvious ways of all by exhibiting celebrities. Celebrities are a great example of people who are willing to embarrass themselves daily in the silly things they have to do in front of the camera and their wide audiences in order to gain fame and fortune to them. Not only are they willing to be silly but they are also trailblazers and unapologetic in what they say and do in front of people.

Madonna and Prince are examples of two people who went to the extreme in their unapologetic and risqué fashion statements in what they wore (and still wear in the case of Madonna). Additionally, celebrities don't care about the negative attention they receive in their anti- aging cosmetic procedures that went wrong for them or for the raunchy and nasty day time shows that they host. They don't care about the negative steam they get from the media and other celebrities when they are making tens of millions of dollars to them. It is for these reasons that you too should not care when you will have to be silly in what you do to become wealthy. So now how can normal people like you and me be silly when it comes to our get rich enterprises? Let's look at some more average everyday people and see what sorts of things that they do that could make them look or feel silly.

People who get rich are willing to go outside of their comfort zones to promote themselves and their businesses or ideas to people. They have to be willing to go big in commercializing real things of value and interest to people and willing to go under the spotlight in front of millions of people. Along with the extreme attention they can attract, they must also be open to any fierce criticism that they may get and be willing to fail in front of people thousands of times as they aspire at their dreams and desires. Rich people are also very aggressive about what they declare to the world in what they are going to do. I told a co-worker of mine back in 2005 that I was going to be a billionaire someday in which he gave me a look of scorn. Do you think I care eighteen years later that I'm not a billionaire? Heck no! I still have bragging rights as a very successful person over someone who is still only making fifty thousand dollars a year as of this day and can't even afford the apartment he is in.

Being silly on your online resume can also open lots of doors for you. At one point, I had labeled myself as a CEO of my own company and that I was a book author in which I listed a bunch of really silly book titles on my page. Although my page was really meant to be just for me, I became embarrassed when I saw other people viewing my page. However, updating my page with all of these things opened my mind up on my book writing endeavors and steered me toward adding positions to my resume that attracted potentially lucrative job offers. One thing I have to mention here is that you can't add any job titles or descriptions to your resume or profile on job posting sites that are not true and valid or else you can be subject to being an imposter so make sure to only add what is true to you. I actually did found and owned my own company and therefore could list myself as a CEO of it.

Those who seek to become wealthy just do without questioning themselves or the process. Sometimes we just have to simply put ourselves out there in which the rest will come to you, and don't care how silly you look or feel because silly is what we have to do to become wealthy. I had to be willing to stick my neck out there in pitching business ideas to even the most prestigious capital venture firms which then brought me to contacting other prestigious people to invest in.

So when it comes to striving for your millionaire status, be willing to be silly in everything you do from the ventures you pursue and how you pursue them as well as what you tell people you are going to do. Don't care about any embarrassment because sometimes embarrassment pays the most when you can go outside the norm of what everyone else is doing to find the things that will bring millions or in some cases, billions of dollars to you. Now before we get to the number one secret to wealth, we will go over the steep sacrifices wealthy people make in the next wealth principle ahead.

Eli Scott |

Wealth Principle 20

Why some celebrities never fix their teeth (and shouldn't)

Wealth consists not in having great possessions, but in having few wants. –Epictetus

In several of the wealth principles in this book, I mentioned that you must go to the extreme in the steep sacrifices you must make in order to become wealthy. While you may think you know what going to the extreme looks like in doing this, many wealthy people make no exception to this. In order to show case the sacrifices that some people make, I would like to discuss one unnamed celebrity who I can personally relate to in why they over the course of their successful and public career never fixed their teeth. To this day, I have yet to get my own teeth straightened and cosmetically whitened as an adult. However, it was not only my teeth that I ignored, but that of a severe toe nail fungus that I had for fifteen years before I finally got that fixed as of a year ago from this writing. Now I do have to interrupt for just a moment and state that I am breaking a number one rule in book writing which is that you never ever write about toe nail fungus and people who have it in any of your books whether fiction or non-fiction, and so this is probably the only time this rule can be broken in book writing which is to share what rich people do that poor people don't in order to become successfully wealthy. And furthermore, my story does have a happy ending where I now have my pretty toe nails back. But back to the moral of this story is that wealthy people have to ignore the things that will get in the way of becoming wealthy including cosmetic procedures.

So now you're probably saying yeah right, there are plenty of celebrities who are massively successful and have cosmetic procedures done all the time in which I will say that those are the people who didn't need to worry about those things distracting them because they had a "guaranteed" path to wealth and some of them are required to have those cosmetic procedures done in order to continue on their paths. Cosmetics are amongst the most time consuming tasks and to have let myself be distracted from the amount of time and attention it takes to fix those problems would have not allowed me to be where I am at today because I needed every waking second of every day to become very successful. If you think you can do cosmetic procedures and still be wealthy someday then have at it, but this book is for the losers, the ones who don't have realistic ways to become wealthy and no ongoing high earning income in which you should ignore any distractions.

Now there is another reason that some very rich people never get cosmetic procedures done which is the opportunity cost or cost benefit in doing so. What do I mean by that? Wealthy people don't spend money on anything that can hold them back monetarily from putting that money into other investment and wealth opportunities. You can choose not to listen to me if you want to but I am coming from the account of what several wealthy people do and if I were me, I'm going to do what wealthy people do and not what poor people do if I want to be wealthy someday. If I had gotten my teeth fixed sooner in life, I guarantee that I would not have ever been able to be as successful as I am in my private high net worth investments as these require an investment minimum of twenty-five thousand to one hundred thousand dollars or more. Spending five to ten grand would have made me miss out on this wealth opportunity by spending too much money on other things.

This is also why rich people are very thrifty with everything from buying all generic products, driving the most economic cars, to buying the lowest budget electronics and appliances. I had the option to either buy a vehicle with a sunroof and fancy dashboard with a touchscreen GPS and radio system or the basic bottom of the line economy car with no sunroof and a regular basic dashboard for five thousand dollars less when I bought my car. Which one do you think I bought. Of course the economy car. I have also written all of my published books not on a laptop or a computer, but on my budget smartphone because I can't afford the opportunity it would cost me to buy a fancy laptop or expensive phone to write this on and my last cheap laptop broke in which I see the opportunity cost in replacing it. This opportunity cost is the same reason that I never went on any vacations in my life until after I was much older and also why I didn't buy into any subscriptions or streaming services. I also shop around for the cheapest cell phone plans, the cheapest mechanics, the cheapest insurance plans, and the cheapest of anything. I am not saying that I trade quality or safety with any of these things. My budget phone and cell phone carrier compete with the highest end phones and services. And I never undercut auto mechanics on labor costs, but I refuse to be gouged on parts.

Along with that, ignoring your cosmetic problems in order to become wealthy does not mean you should ignore the doctor or the dentist. I still got my teeth checked and cleaned annually throughout my endeavors. I also went to the doctor regularly to make sure I was healthy and that none of my cosmetic problems were the result of any underlying conditions that were a threat to my health. While rich people sacrifice cosmetics and their vanity due to the opportunity cost, there is certainly no benefit to gain if you don't have your health!

Before I end here, I will also say that there are people who will say that it's stupid and unrealistic to be thrifty with your money, because we need to spend in order to keep the economy going. My response to that is that these are the same people who are rich and whose income relies on ninety nine percent of the populations spending to them. These are also the same people who are money pinchers in order to stay massively wealthy. Additionally, only one percent of the people who read this book will follow these with principles in which the rest will keep the economy going. If you are one of the few who wants to be wealthy, you need to save your money that you can then leverage which will then allow you to spend more money on businesses and good causes if you want to. Saving and being thrifty with your money also has it's special place in the economy to protect us from large scale financial disaster as well as your own financial disaster, which is why there are still experts who advise on how to save and where and what not to buy such as cars appliances and homes during down times.

In reflection, I am glad I chose to ignore my cosmetic needs and was thrifty with my money because now I can do what I want and be on vacation for the rest of my life. What you do is your choice and it's up to you to decide what steps you want to take to become the winner in this game. However, if you are still with me, then you will understand the number one secret to wealth ahead.

Eli Scott |

The Number One Secret to Wealth

The best way to predict the future is to create it. -Abraham Lincoln

It is never too late to be what you might have been. -George Eliot

Twenty years from now you will be more disappointed by the things that you didn't do than by the ones you did do. —Mark Twain

While this last key to your success is a wealth principle in itself, it is the ultimate hidden treasure in amassing your fortune for you and that is only you can make you wealthy. I know there are some cynics here who are going to sarcastically retort to this final wealth principle in that there are lots of people who become wealthy from other things beyond themselves. My response to that is that this book is again for the losers like me who were not born into money. So if you are a loser like me who wants to become wealthy, you are the only one who can make it happen. It is up to you to do anything and everything it takes to get there, from gaining the education or skills you need to then taking the massive action every single day of your life to build your wealth empire.

So now as I mentioned in the introduction, is it really possible to become rich in the next two to five years and how? Those who become rich don't have limited mindsets and find the careers or hustles that pay as well as the high net worth private accredited investments, partnerships, and businesses that can enterprise them. You can't think about the limiting mediocre goals that poor people have and you need to be desirous of and willing to go big in enterprising you. You don't get rich by going small and serving one person at a time, but by leveraging your income by selling to masses of people at once (think apartment rentals, national correspondents, franchising out physical or digital business to other people, selling books, courses, and seminars, and branding or licensing physical or non-physical products).

A golden key to your success with breaking past your limiting beliefs will be to aim high and shoot for the stars to get anything to come back to you. Aiming high then brings us to aiming for the biggest things that will enterprise you first such as that billion dollar idea for you. When you aim as high as you can first then you will find yourself working towards the greatest things that will bring your wealth to you and even if you only end up being worth ten or twenty million with your goals then you are still better off than poor people who only aim for their low paying office jobs.

Finally, those who get rich take action now. If you want to be that mega millionaire superstar or make it to the beaches of Hawaii or just simply have the home and lifestyle that you want, you have to make the decision RIGHT NOW, as in this very moment that you are without a doubt going to be rich someday. Don't save it for tomorrow or maybe in ten years from now when you have your sh** together. If you don't have it together now, you won't in ten years from now either. Your chances of becoming rich decrease significantly if you sit on it and you will be wasting the precious time needed to build and accumulate your wealth for you.

So now knowing how our poor minds work, I can see you saying well of course I am making the decision to become rich now and to do what it takes to get there, but are you really and what does that mean? I knew that this meant that I had to get rid of and separate myself from anyone be it friends, family or romantic partners who were only pulling me down. It meant that I had to throw away everything in my house that wasn't serving me and I had to let go of anything be it comfort and leisure that would only distract me. It meant I had to have the no non-sense attitude and to take action to pursue my wealth for me.

This now brings us to living for the future. While all of your broke friends and family will tell you that it's about living for today, rich people always live for tomorrow. Rich people know that they will be living in their dream home and have their dream car someday, but they don't do it by not working for it now because they won't have it in twenty years from now if they don't do it now. They know that every second of every day is critical in making that dream a reality for them. So you don't make it happen by living in the present moment but by what you have to do today in this very moment to catch up with your future fortune. Therefore, making the decision now and living in the future will be the factors that will determine your future fortune.

If there is any final nugget I can give you in becoming wealthy, it is that those who are willing to take big risks will win at this money making game. I am not ever suggesting that you put your house, your life, or your kids lives on the line in doing so, but, you too will have to be willing to take huge risks in all of your decisions for you. No one leverages their income without doing that in their money-making opportunities for them, and they can do so by mitigating their risk along the way. Even wealthy investors themselves such as those on Shark Tank and Dragons Den are not always impressed by those who risk everything for a chance to become wealthy with their inventions. I took huge risks in my career, real estate, and investment decisions but didn't do so without padding those risks with income and savings in the event that I could lose it all.

Everything it takes to become rich requires practicing and doing everyday no matter how many times you fail doing so. I know this is the most overused analogy but it is the strongest one in which I say it's like being in a batting cage everyday and swinging at the ball over and over until you hit that home run. You have to be an executor against all obstacles and you just have to execute against the difficulty in it all. Becoming a self made millionaire takes a lot of energy, a lot of discipline, a lot of patience, and a lot of learning and doing and there are days when you will lose all hope in what you do. You will feel a lot of loss, a lot of aggravation, a lot of fear, a lot of doubt, a lot of negativity, and furthermore the pain of challenging all that will be ahead of you. There will be days where you will cry, days where you will want to puke, and days where you will feel punched in the stomach through the intensity of it all, and so at the end of the day, becoming rich comes down to only one thing and that one thing is you. It is only you who will make you wealthy. While you think you may know what this means, wealthy people once again take this to the extreme.

What rich people do that poor people don't is that they don't let anything stop them, both literally and figuratively speaking. Rather, they maintain the severe discipline it takes to work at it in which they find their why in doing it. And so I ask, is your bigger why to be stuck in your unhappiness and in pain for the rest of your life as you suffer to pay the bills everyday, or is your bigger why to finally break yourself free, to have the life that you want free of all of the pain? It isn't until your pain is more painful than the work it will take to enterprise you that you will find your reason to do. The golden key to mastering your success is to have unwavering faith and trust in everything you do and to let the music move you.

It is with all of this that I wish you the best in all that you do in finding massive wealth to you.

For those who want the insider secret to internet get rich scams as well as a little more insight on real estate, I provide one more chapter on these two things ahead.

Eli Scott |

The Quick Dirty on Get Rich Schemes and Real Estate

So what is really up with all of these people throwing their pitches at you that they became wealthy or six and seven figure earners with their systems? The reality of this is that while some of them may have gotten rich with these systems, they didn't do so without spending just as much money as they have earned to market their systems. Additionally, they seek to gain wealth not by helping you to get wealthy with their farce systems, but by selling their courses, franchises, and software to you.

Pay close attention to the gurus who try to lure you in with their superficial claims that they got rich with cryptos when they in reality lose on those crypto investments. They use this bait to draw you into their other underlying systems that are meant to make them rich and not you rich. As an example, I came across one person who was luring people in with their lines on how to get rich in cryptos but when digging deeper I found that they were really just trying to sell their new crytpto sports betting system to people.

As I talk about in my other book series, there is no such thing as simply getting rich and you cannot just look for all of the mystical people and their magical formulas on how to get massively wealthy. A lot of these programs are run by people who are selling you a promise at the surface but setting you up for failure beyond that surface. Additionally, many of them are not really meant to make you rich, but to sell you hopes and dreams as they collect thousands of dollars from you. This now brings me to the Old Wise Sage who is a character in Think and Be Rich and the Portal to Financial Gold in which I recite what he has to say to those hopeful entrepreneurs chasing after get rich systems:

"When you rise above the picture, you will see a bunch of mystical creatures who broke down their brick walls to amass their fortune. What you don't see, however, was the difficult journey that they went on and the trials and tribulations that they had in the process. When you rise above the picture, you will see that going straight to the pot of gold is about determining if you are passionate enough to do what these other mystical creatures had to do to get there, and if you are willing to go through what they had to. As you set out on your endeavors, you will see that getting rich is not about plugging into all of these systems that you think will just spit back gold, or about pursuing wealth systems that are known to be risky. While these systems can be proven for some, they are not proven for everybody. When others want to preach that it comes down to how you think or as simple as allowing yourself to be wealthy, you rise further above the picture to see that your success with any get rich enterprise, is fully based on your performance in physically pursuing and executing systems."

So now what does that all mean? It means that getting rich is not quick or easy. There is no such thing as the mystical phenomena of those who simply get rich unless they were born into money. These various get rich gurus will tell you that you cannot expect to get rich over night and that you need to work hard at an endeavor for the next ten years in order to become rich. My response is yes you do, but don't waste your time and money on the wrong systems that still have all of these barriers and sucking in your monthly subscriptions in which you seek the real and proven ways to become wealthy. Additionally, these same programs sell audio courses on how to change your mindset to a positive one in hustling their system. The only thing "how to get rich" books and audios have taught me is how to not have fear and doubt, but they do not circumvent the many barriers to entrepreneurial success. Get rich programs and schemes will preach that going to school, not investing money into a business, and not investing into your get rich education are "poor" choices to make in life. At the end of the day, you will be even more poor by giving your money away to these money draining systems!

Those who simply get rich do not endlessly pull out their credit cards to invest in get rich systems that never spit back money. Rather, they pursue the things in which they can start the entire enterprise for free or gain the right investors to back them and don't throw in even one penny into anything until they have thoroughly researched everything and determined that it is viable. A smart and proven entrepreneur will determine everything that it takes for a business to be lucrative, and while one path may seem to be different than the last, a lot of these businesses are up against the same barriers and pitfalls to their success. And so again, these programs try to lure people in with their get rich value proposition and most of them are not at all transparent about product viability and what it actually takes to run the business.

It doesn't matter if it is about real estate, cryptocurrencies, trading, affiliate marketing, drop shipping, franchising, or you name it, they all require a ton

of everything you don't want to put into it which is your time and money.
They also have the main money-making machine hidden behind them which is
to sell you education courses and programs rather than the value proposition
they sell you in making you rich and wealthy. A couple examples I have come
across with this are those who lure you in with getting rich on investments,
cryptocurrencies, and real estate in order to sell their books, gambling sites, and
real estate software to you.

Now who am I to talk about real estate and its potential? While I am not a
real estate tycoon, broker, or lawyer, what I can say is that I don't need to be any
of these people to point out facts. Real estate has been known to be tricky for
many and has thrown a few tycoons into bankruptcy. I also know someone near
and dear to me who was such a real estate tycoon with a massive portfolio at one
point who lost out on over half a million dollars on their real estate portfolio
during the COVID-19 pandemic which no one in the world saw coming. It's
in the what you don't know in what could happen at any time that can sweep
you away in its destructive path.

As many wealth experts advise, you are taking a lot of risk when buying
into any type of real estate crowdfunding whether it's residential or commercial
because you are up against the ebb and flow of the markets, rising interest rates,
opposing buying and selling strategies between you and the management team,
and poor management itself that can completely fail in making these winning
opportunities. Real estate crowdfunding platforms are so extremely risky that
even wealthy people and other real estate tycoons themselves worth hundreds
of millions or billions of dollars won't even invest in them or fund them. As
they say you should diversify your investments, this includes real estate in your
investing or money-making opportunities.

If you are going to invest in or buy any type of real estate investment vehicle
or property including your primary home, do not do so without speaking to
qualified licensed brokers and lawyers who are the only ones that are qualified
to guide you on the best instruments and real estate opportunities for you.
On top of the risk involved in any real estate purchase, people have found
themselves to be upside down on the purchase of their homes that they cannot
resell their homes when home developers find loopholes in legal requirements
to sell them. Look up the 2022-2023 water requirement loophole in the sales
of Arizona homes as an example. These poor people bought homes from

developers who found loopholes in the one hundred year water requirements to sell them in which the state had to shut off water to these homes when they couldn't supply it, leaving these people in a dilemma between high water bills and not being able to sell their homes.

So going back to get rich systems, it doesn't matter why some people succeed with them and why some people don't. What matters is when you need to realize it's not possible or feasible for you and when you seek the thing that will enterprise you. If you are looking to start any kind of business, consider looking into those with high profit margins and least cost of goods sold and overhead to them such as digital products and services. Cost of goods sold or COGS is the cost of storing and selling inventory (products) as well as the losses incurred on those not sold, which is why they can carry low profit margins to them. As with anything you set out to do, be very discerning with looking deep into the reality of such enterprises by researching them before embarking on them in which I highly suggest you simply look for the realistic ways to become wealthy and to learn how to leverage your money.

Eli Scott |

www.ingramcontent.com/pod-product-compliance
Lightning Source LLC
LaVergne TN
LVHW051135080426
835510LV00018B/2435

Table of Contents